D1498082

Transfer Between Courts

Institute of Judicial Administration

American Bar Association

Juvenile Justice Standards

STANDARDS RELATING TO

Transfer Between Courts

Recommended by the
IJA-ABA JOINT COMMISSION ON JUVENILE JUSTICE STANDARDS

Hon. Irving R. Kaufman, *Chairman*

Approved by the
HOUSE OF DELEGATES, AMERICAN BAR ASSOCIATION, 1979

Charles Z. Smith, *Chairman of Drafting Committee II*
Charles Whitebread, *Reporter*
Michael H. Tonry, *Special Editor*

Ballinger Publishing Company ● Cambridge, Massachusetts
A Subsidiary of Harper & Row, Publishers, Inc.

DRAFTING COMMITTEE II—COURT ROLES AND PROCEDURES

This document was prepared for the Juvenile Justice Standards Project of the Institute of Judicial Administration and the American Bar Association. The project is supported by grants prepared under Grant Numbers 71-NI-99-0014; 72-NI-99-0032; 74-NI-99-0043; and 75-NI-99-0101 from the National Institute of Criminal Justice and Law Enforcement, and 76-JN-99-0018; 78-JN-AX-0002; and 79-JN-AX-0025 from the National Institute of Juvenile Justice and Delinquency Prevention, Office of Juvenile Justice and Delinquency Prevention, Law Enforcement Assistance Administration, U.S. Department of Justice, the American Bar Endowment, the Andrew W. Mellon Foundation, the Vincent Astor Foundation, and the Herman Goldman Foundation. The views expressed in this draft do not represent positions taken by the funding sources. Votes on the standards were unanimous in most but not all cases. Specific objections by individual members of the IJA-ABA Joint Commission have been noted in formal dissents printed in the volumes concerned.

Library of Congress Cataloging in Publication Data

Whitebread, Charles.
   Standards relating to transfer between courts.

   At head of title: Institute of Judicial Administration—American Bar Association Juvenile Justice Standards Project.
   "Approved by the IJA-ABA Joint Commission on Juvenile Justice Standards . . . and Drafting Committee II—Court Roles and Procedures."
   Includes bibliographical references.
   1. Juvenile courts—United States. 2. Criminal courts—United States. 3. Jurisdiction—United States. I. Juvenile Justice Standards Project. II. Title. III. Title: Transfer between courts.
KF9709.W5   345'.73'08   76-17798
ISBN 0-88410-230-0

Preface

The standards and commentary in this volume are part of a series designed to cover the spectrum of problems pertaining to the laws affecting children. They examine the juvenile justice system and its relationship to the rights and responsibilities of juveniles. The series was prepared under the supervision of a Joint Commission on Juvenile Justice Standards appointed by the Institute of Judicial Administration and the American Bar Association. Seventeen volumes in the series were approved by the House of Delegates of the American Bar Association on February 12, 1979.

The standards are intended to serve as guidelines for action by legislators, judges, administrators, public and private agencies, local civic groups, and others responsible for or concerned with the treatment of youths at local, state, and federal levels. The twenty-three volumes issued by the joint commission cover the entire field of juvenile justice administration, including the jurisdiction and organization of trial and appellate courts hearing matters concerning juveniles; the transfer of jurisdiction to adult criminal courts; and the functions performed by law enforcement officers and court intake, probation, and corrections personnel. Standards for attorneys representing the state, for juveniles and their families, and for the procedures to be followed at the preadjudication, adjudication, disposition, and postdisposition stages are included. One volume in this series sets forth standards for the statutory classification of delinquent acts and the rules governing the sanctions to be imposed. Other volumes deal with problems affecting nondelinquent youth, including recommendations concerning the permissible range of intervention by the state in cases of abuse or neglect, status offenses (such as truancy and running away), and contractual, medical, educational, and employment rights of minors.

The history of the Juvenile Justice Standards Project illustrates the breadth and scope of its task. In 1971, the Institute of Judicial Administration, a private, nonprofit research and educational organization located at New York University School of Law, began planning the Juvenile Justice Standards Project. At that time, the Project on Standards for Criminal Justice of the ABA, initiated by IJA seven years earlier, was completing the last of twelve volumes of recommendations for the adult criminal justice system. However, those standards were not designed to address the issues confronted by the separate courts handling juvenile matters. The Juvenile Justice Standards Project was created to consider those issues.

A planning committee chaired by then Judge and now Chief Judge Irving R. Kaufman of the United States Court of Appeals for the Second Circuit met in October 1971. That winter, reporters who would be responsible for drafting the volumes met with six planning subcommittees to identify and analyze the important issues in the juvenile justice field. Based on material developed by them, the planning committee charted the areas to be covered.

In February 1973, the ABA became a co-sponsor of the project. IJA continued to serve as the secretariat of the project. The IJA-ABA Joint Commission on Juvenile Justice Standards was then created to serve as the project's governing body. The joint commission, chaired by Chief Judge Kaufman, consists of twenty-nine members, approximately half of whom are lawyers and judges, the balance representing nonlegal disciplines such as psychology and sociology. The chairpersons of the four drafting committees also serve on the joint commission. The perspective of minority groups was introduced by a Minority Group Advisory Committee established in 1973, members of which subsequently joined the commission and the drafting committees. David Gilman has been the director of the project since July 1976.

The task of writing standards and accompanying commentary was undertaken by more than thirty scholars, each of whom was assigned a topic within the jurisdiction of one of the four advisory drafting committees: Committee I, Intervention in the Lives of Children; Committee II, Court Roles and Procedures; Committee III, Treatment and Correction; and Committee IV, Administration. The committees were composed of more than 100 members chosen for their background and experience not only in legal issues affecting youth, but also in related fields such as psychiatry, psychology, sociology, social work, education, corrections, and police work. The standards and commentary produced by the reporters and drafting committees were presented to the IJA-ABA Joint Commission on Juvenile Justice Standards for consideration. The deliberations of the joint commission led to revisions in the standards and commentary presented to them, culminating in the published tentative drafts.

The published tentative drafts were distributed widely to members of the legal community, juvenile justice specialists, and organizations directly concerned with the juvenile justice system for study and comment. The ABA assigned the task of reviewing individual volumes to ABA sections whose members are expert in the specific areas covered by those volumes. Especially helpful during this review period were the comments, observations, and guidance provided by Professor Livingston Hall, Chairperson, Committee on Juvenile Justice of the Section of Criminal Justice, and Marjorie M. Childs, Chairperson of the Juvenile Justice Standards Review Committee of the Section of Family Law of the ABA. The recommendations submitted to the project by the professional groups, attorneys, judges, and ABA sections were presented to an executive committee of the joint commission, to whom the responsibility of responding had been delegated by the full commission. The executive committee consisted of the following members of the joint commission:

Chief Judge Irving R. Kaufman, *Chairman*
Hon. William S. Fort, *Vice Chairman*
Prof. Charles Z. Smith, *Vice Chairman*
Dr. Eli Bower
Allen Breed
William T. Gossett, Esq.
Robert W. Meserve, Esq.
Milton G. Rector
Daniel L. Skoler, Esq.
Hon. William S. White
Hon. Patricia M. Wald, *Special Consultant*

The executive committee met in 1977 and 1978 to discuss the proposed changes in the published standards and commentary. Minutes issued after the meetings reflecting the decisions by the executive committee were circulated to the members of the joint commission and the ABA House of Delegates, as well as to those who had transmitted comments to the project.

On February 12, 1979, the ABA House of Delegates approved seventeen of the twenty-three published volumes. It was understood that the approved volumes would be revised to conform to the changes described in the minutes of the 1977 and 1978 executive committee meetings. The *Schools and Education* volume was not presented to the House and the five remaining volumes—*Abuse and Neglect, Court Organization and Administration, Juvenile Delinquency and Sanctions, Juvenile Probation Function*, and *Noncriminal*

Misbehavior—were held over for final consideration at the 1980 mid-winter meeting of the House.

Among the agreed-upon changes in the standards was the decision to bracket all numbers limiting time periods and sizes of facilities in order to distinguish precatory from mandatory standards and thereby allow for variations imposed by differences among jurisdictions. In some cases, numerical limitations concerning a juvenile's age also are bracketed.

The tentative drafts of the seventeen volumes approved by the ABA House of Delegates in February 1979, revised as agreed, are now ready for consideration and implementation by the components of the juvenile justice system in the various states and localities.

Much time has elapsed from the start of the project to the present date and significant changes have taken place both in the law and the social climate affecting juvenile justice in this country. Some of the changes are directly traceable to these standards and the intense national interest surrounding their promulgation. Other major changes are the indirect result of the standards; still others derive from independent local influences, such as increases in reported crime rates.

The volumes could not be revised to reflect legal and social developments subsequent to the drafting and release of the tentative drafts in 1975 and 1976 without distorting the context in which they were written and adopted. Therefore, changes in the standards or commentary dictated by the decisions of the executive committee subsequent to the publication of the tentative drafts are indicated in a special notation at the front of each volume.

In addition, the series will be brought up to date in the revised version of the summary volume, *Standards for Juvenile Justice: A Summary and Analysis*, which will describe current history, major trends, and the observable impact of the proposed standards on the juvenile justice system from their earliest dissemination. Far from being outdated, the published standards have become guideposts to the future of juvenile law.

The planning phase of the project was supported by a grant from the National Institute of Law Enforcement and Criminal Justice of the Law Enforcement Assistance Administration. The National Institute also supported the drafting phase of the project, with additional support from grants from the American Bar Endowment, and the Andrew Mellon, Vincent Astor, and Herman Goldman foundations. Both the National Institute and the American Bar Endowment funded the final revision phase of the project.

An account of the history and accomplishments of the project would not be complete without acknowledging the work of some of the people who, although no longer with the project, contributed immeasurably to its achievements. Orison Marden, a former president of the ABA, was co-chairman of the commission from 1974 until his death in August 1975. Paul Nejelski was director of the project during its planning phase from 1971 to 1973. Lawrence Schultz, who was research director from the inception of the project, was director from 1973 until 1974. From 1974 to 1975, Delmar Karlen served as vice-chairman of the commission and as chairman of its executive committee, and Wayne Mucci was director of the project. Barbara Flicker was director of the project from 1975 to 1976. Justice Tom C. Clark was chairman for ABA liaison from 1975 to 1977.

Legal editors included Jo Rena Adams, Paula Ryan, and Ken Taymor. Other valued staff members were Fred Cohen, Pat Pickrell, Peter Garlock, and Oscar Garcia-Rivera. Mary Anne O'Dea and Susan J. Sandler also served as editors. Amy Berlin and Kathy Kolar were research associates. Jennifer K. Schweickart and Ramelle Cochrane Pulitzer were editorial assistants.

It should be noted that the positions adopted by the joint commission and stated in these volumes do not represent the official policies or views of the organizations with which the members of the joint commission and the drafting committees are associated.

This volume is part of a series of standards and commentary prepared under the supervision of Drafting Committee II, which also includes the following volumes:

COURT ORGANIZATION AND ADMINISTRATION
COUNSEL FOR PRIVATE PARTIES
PROSECUTION
THE JUVENILE PROBATION FUNCTION: INTAKE AND PRE-
    DISPOSITION INVESTIGATIVE SERVICES
PRETRIAL COURT PROCEEDINGS
ADJUDICATION
APPEALS AND COLLATERAL REVIEW

Addendum
of
Revisions in the 1977 Tentative Draft

As discussed in the Preface, the published tentative drafts were distributed to the appropriate ABA sections and other interested individuals and organizations. Comments and suggestions concerning the volumes were solicited by the executive committee of the IJA-ABA Joint Commission. The executive committee then reviewed the standards and commentary within the context of the recommendations received and adopted certain modifications. The specific changes affecting this volume are set forth below. Corrections in form, spelling, or punctuation are not included in this enumeration.

1. Standards 1.1 B. and 1.1 C. were amended by reducing the minimum age for criminal court jurisdiction from over fifteen to over fourteen years of age at the time the offense is alleged to have occurred.

The commentaries to Standards 1.1 B. and 1.1 C. also were revised to include fifteen-year-old juveniles among those under eighteen who could be subject to waiver of juvenile court jurisdiction.

2. Standard 1.2 A. was amended by bracketing thirty-six months to comply with the policy adopted by the executive committee of making recommended time limitations permissive rather than mandatory.

The commentary to Standard 1.2 A. also was revised to place brackets around three years, the recommended maximum duration for juvenile court dispositions.

3. The commentary to Standard 1.2 B. was revised to add two sentences at the end of the last paragraph to expand the cross-reference to the provisions in the *Dispositions* volume that modify a disposition by applying *Dispositions* Standard 5.4 to revocation of probation.

4. Standards 2.1 A. through 2.1 E. were amended to bracket all numbers representing time limits, adding class two juvenile offenses

to the category of charges for which waiver of juvenile court jurisdiction would be possible, and reducing to fifteen the age at which the alleged juvenile offense must have been committed for waiver to be possible.

The commentaries to Standards 2.1 A. through 2.1 E. were revised to reflect the above changes.

5. Standard 2.2 A. 1. was amended to add class two offenses to the provision requiring a finding of probable cause as a prerequisite to waiver.

The commentary also was revised to add class two offenses.

6. Standard 2.2 C. was amended by adding class two offenses to the provisions on necessary findings for waiver, by requiring a finding of a prior record of adjudication for class two offenses only, and by adding a cross-reference to Standard 2.1 E. providing that the court's finding that the juvenile is not a proper person for juvenile court handling must be in writing.

The commentary to Standard 2.2 C. was revised accordingly.

7. Standard 2.2 D. was amended to include class two offenses in the provision on the substitution of a finding of probable cause in subsequent juvenile court proceedings but not in any subsequent criminal proceeding.

8. Standards 2.3 A. and B. were amended to bracket five court days for notice of the waiver hearing.

9. Standard 2.3 C. was amended to add to the provision that the court pay expert witness fees and expenses a clause making payment subject to the court finding the expert testimony necessary.

The commentary was revised to include the same caveat.

10. Standard 2.3 E. was amended to add class two offenses to the provision placing the burden of proof of probable cause and of the juvenile's unfitness for juvenile court handling on the prosecutor.

Commentary to Standard 2.3 E. was revised to add to the discussion of the juvenile's right to challenge prosecution evidence a cross-reference to the right to compulsory process in *Dispositional Procedures* Standard 6.2, *Juvenile Records and Information Systems* Standard 5.7 B., and *Pretrial Court Proceedings* Standard 1.5 F.

11. Standard 2.3 I. was amended to delete "criminal," thereby extending the inadmissibility of admissions by the juvenile during the waiver hearing to both juvenile and criminal proceedings, and to add an exception for perjury proceedings.

12. Standard 2.4 was amended to bracket the seven days for filing appeals.

Commentary to Standard 2.4 was revised to add a cross-reference to *Appeals and Collateral Review* Standard 2.2, which authorizes appeal of the waiver decision by either party.

Contents

Introduction

Drawing lines is difficult and necessarily arbitrary. The line between "adult" and "child" is important in every context, but nowhere more than in the application of the criminal law. The "adult" faces the processes and sanctions of the criminal court. The "child" experiences the juvenile court, its treatment programs, and limited penalties.

This volume is about waiver, the process by which the juvenile court releases certain juveniles from its jurisdiction and transfers them to the criminal courts.

Juvenile courts exist because Americans admit to a fundamental difference between children and adults. We are, perhaps, more sympathetic to troublesome children than to criminal adults. Because they are immature and not held to the same degree of responsibility for their acts, or because they are more malleable and susceptible to rehabilitation, children are brought within the jurisdiction of a juvenile court whose rhetoric, and sometimes whose practice, is kinder, more hopeful, and less vindictive than that of the criminal court.

The juvenile court is often described as a child-saving institution, principally rehabilitative. By contrast, the criminal court acknowledges its multiple purposes of retribution, deterrence, containment, and, when it can be reconciled with the others, rehabilitation. Public opinion appears to tolerate, even endorse, the propositions that juvenile courts should be different from criminal courts and that children should be treated more benevolently than adults. The juvenile court's clients are usually referred to in this volume asexually and unemotionally as "juveniles" or "persons." In these few paragraphs, however, we use the terms "children" and "child" advisedly. A "child" is not an adult, and the line between them must be drawn somewhere.

Many American jurisdictions have determined in recent years that an eighteen-year-old is an adult for purposes of voting, conscription, marriage, and alcohol consumption. An adult for some purposes, the argument goes, should be an adult for all. Eighteen years of age will suffice to draw the line for crime as for alcohol or the ballot.

1

There is nothing inherently right or just about a line drawn at eighteen. Other ages would do as well, and have. Professor Egon Bittner has convincingly argued that the concept of adolescence is a recent Western invention. "Policing Juveniles—The Social Bases of Common Practice," in *Pursuing Justice for the Child* (Rosenheim ed. 1976). See also J.R. Gillis, *Youth and History: Tradition and Change in European Age Relations, 1770-Present* (1975). Without adolescence, the child-adult line might be at fourteen, or thirteen, or younger.

No matter what the age, difficult cases will remain. There always will be individuals who are victims of arbitrary lines. Innocent and immature adults of eighteen years will be processed by the criminal courts. "Young person" or "young adult" programs may be available which will mean exposure to lesser sanctions than face other adults, but they will be in the criminal courts just the same. A compassionate prosecutor or judge may exercise discretion in favor of a particular defendant, but that will be fortuitous. Beneficence will be good fortune, not a theoretical right. Whatever the qualities of children which argue for special treatment, an eighteen-year-old, by irrebuttable legal presumption, is not a child. Neither the laws of any state nor this volume propose any method by which the presumption of adulthood can be overcome.*

The converse problem ought to be equally easy. A tough-minded view of majority might have as a logical corollary a soft-hearted view of minority. If an adult is outside the juvenile court's jurisdiction because the alleged act occurred a day past his or her eighteenth birthday, a child should be within the juvenile court if the act occurs a day before the crucial birthday.

It doesn't work that way. The presumption of childhood can be rebutted in almost every state. Under certain circumstances, children of certain ages who have allegedly committed certain acts can be transferred to the criminal court. This volume offers specific guides to making transfer decisions. It discusses who decides, under whose initiatives these decisions are made, what procedures and information are involved, age range, and the nature of the decision-making mechanisms.

The stakes are high. The adult accused of murder, rape, or armed robbery can be punished with life imprisonment in most jurisdictions, in some with death. In most cases the child faces punishments of lesser duration and severity.

---

*The unusual process of reverse certification—see *Ark. Stat.* § 45-241 (1964) and *Vt. Stat. Ann.* tit. 33, § 635(b) (Supp. 9, 1974)—by which juveniles first appear in criminal court and the criminal court judge determines whether juvenile court jurisdiction is appropriate, may be an exception.

If something about children compels the existence of juvenile courts, the lack of symmetry between the irrebuttable presumption of majority and the rebuttable presumption of minority should be disturbing. But, disturbing or not, the possibility of waiver is unavoidable. Some acts are so offensive to the community that the arbitrary line drawn at eighteen cannot acceptably be used to protect the alleged wrongdoer. The serious offender should not be permitted to escape the criminal justice system simply because he or she is a day or a year short of eighteen. As age eighteen approaches, credible argument can be made that the juvenile court's always inadequate resources should not be devoted to those youthful wrongdoers whose offenses are so serious or who appear to be so incorrigible as to be unworthy of or beyond help.

Finally, all court proceedings are prospective. They deal with past acts but also with future remedies, sanctions, and programs. If the conduct alleged is sufficiently serious, some mechanism should exist to permit retention of authority over some juveniles beyond the eighteenth birthday. A waiver decision will determine which court will have jurisdiction. If the precipitating acts are serious enough, the criminal court's capacity to maintain control over the juvenile for long periods of time may be more appropriate and socially reassuring than the maximum three-year period of juvenile court control proposed in these standards.

The standards that follow express a preference for retention by the juvenile court of jurisdiction over most persons under eighteen. An implicit presumption should be made explicit; every person under eighteen years of age at the time he or she commits an act that would constitute a criminal offense should remain subject to the juvenile court's jurisdiction unless every one of many conditions is present. Every procedural and substantive standard that follows grows out of that presumption.

The presumption in favor of juvenile court jurisdiction need not adopt any particular theoretical rationale for the juvenile court and the concept of separate treatment for juveniles. One rationale, the first principle of the juvenile court, is that children are qualitatively different from adults. Possibly they are more innocent and in some moral sense less responsible for their acts and more deserving of compassion than are adults. Possibly they are victims of criminogenic environments from which they should be given every opportunity to escape. Possibly children are more malleable than adults and more likely to benefit from gentler handling. For these reasons and others, it can be argued that, whenever possible, children should be accorded a humane, compassionate response to their disturbing acts.

A second rationale for the juvenile court derives from the view recently summarized as radical nonintervention. This view, in broadest outline (it takes many forms) is that many young people engage in seriously antisocial acts, but most simply outgrow them. Arguing in part from labeling theories, this view urges that the children who are least likely to mature out of antisocial acts are those who are identified as delinquent and treated as such by the state (and necessarily the community at large). Most juvenile acts by this view ought to be disregarded. Moreover, the juvenile and criminal justice systems disproportionately enforce laws against the poor and dispossessed who are accordingly labeled "delinquent" and eventually, by self-fulfilling prophecy, become adult criminal statistics. While some violent, threatening, or repetitive acts cannot conscientiously be ignored, radical nonintervention argues for the minimum possible intervention in children's lives. The juvenile court often has lesser consequences (if only because the duration and severity of its sanctions are more limited, and because its records are, ostensibly, confidential) than the criminal court and should therefore be preferred.

A third rationale is that the juvenile court is peculiarly capable of rehabilitating disruptive or disturbed children. Recent research urges skepticism about the efficacy of existing rehabilitative methods. Stanton Wheeler in 1966 summarized juvenile rehabilitative programs and concluded:

> But do we know enough about delinquency to specify the ways in which even a moderate reduction could be brought about? In terms of verified knowledge, the answer must be an unqualified no. . . . Indeed, as of now, there are no demonstrable and proven methods for reducing the incidence of serious delinquent acts through preventive or rehabilitative procedures. Either the descriptive knowledge has not been translated into feasible action programs, or the programs have not been successfully implemented; or if implemented, they have lacked evaluation; or if evaluated, the results usually have been negative; and in the few cases of reported positive results, replications have been lacking. Wheeler et al., "Juvenile Delinquency—Its Prevention and Control," in President's Commission on Law Enforcement and Administration of Justice, *Task Force Report: Juvenile Delinquency and Youth Crime* 410 (1967).

In 1973, LaMar Empey canvassed the major experiments in rehabilitation of delinquent children and concluded:

> [S]pecial treatment institutions for juveniles have been built, but

ironically, they seem to have perpetuated many of the same difficulties [as adult institutions]. Except for the protection of society in the most extreme cases, there is little evidence to support the notion that juvenile institutions are successful. "Diversion, Due Process and Deinstitutionalization," in *Prisoners in America* 35 (Ohlin ed. 1973).

Paul Lerman's 1974 reanalysis of the evaluation data of two of the most acclaimed juvenile rehabilitative programs concluded: "There is an array of evidence that current correctional 'packages,' regardless of their contents, are relatively ineffective in changing youth behavior." *Community Treatment and Social Control—A Critical Analysis of Juvenile Policy* 96 (1974). "It is . . . evident that an effective juvenile control/treatment strategy has yet to be scientifically demonstrated." *Id.* at 206.

Probably the most that can be said presently is that lavishly funded experimental programs with a high level of staff commitment, low staff-client ratios, and empathetic long-term aftercare facilities have some likelihood of improving the life chances of the children who experience them. We can hope that rehabilitative programs will be successful. We do not know that we can improve life chances, but we need not yet be convinced that we cannot. The possibility that juveniles are more susceptible of rehabilitation is not to be dismissed or belittled. Many of those involved in the creation of the juvenile court and in its present administration have believed in its promise. To the extent that the juvenile court is successful with some children and changes some lives for the better, the rehabilitative argument for the juvenile court has great moral force.

Each of the first three rationales is vulnerable to serious objections. To the first, it can be argued, as Justice Fortas did in *In re Gault*, 387 U.S. 1 (1967), that we have failed to deliver to the child as we promised and that nonadult characteristics do not justify the juvenile court's reduced protections and the juvenile's vulnerability to unstructured judicial and social worker discretion. That view has been widely adopted. Witness the many recent calls for limitation of the juvenile court's criminal jurisdiction to acts that would be criminal if committed by an adult and for adoption by the juvenile court of most of the procedural protections of the criminal court for juvenile offenders. Other volumes in these standards support that position.

The second rationale is convincing only to those (who are increasing in number but still a minority) who accept most of the tenets of radical nonintervention and who further accept the proposition that a criminal court intervention will cause more harm than a juvenile court intervention.

The rehabilitative rationale by itself is persuasive only to the optimistic at heart and to that dwindling number of informed people who believe that the technology of rehabilitation has achieved a reliability that justifies taking special power over others to change them.

A fourth rationale for the juvenile court remains and it may be the most compelling of all. Assume that children are not, or morally should not be viewed as, materially different from adults. Assume that innate difference is not a compelling justification for the separate juvenile court. Assume that the criminal court's social consequences are no more severe than those of the juvenile court. Assume further a negative or agnostic view of the technology of rehabilitation.

The fourth rationale is that the criminal justice system is so inhumane, so poorly financed and staffed, and so generally destructive that the juvenile court cannot do worse. Perhaps it can do better. This type of cynical analysis, often called a theory of less harm, has appeared in many contexts in recent years. Plans for new prisons have been justified on the basis that they will cause less harm to their inmates than do existing megaprisons. The influential *Beyond the Best Interests of the Child* (Goldstein, Freud, and Solnit [1973]) calls for employment of a "least detrimental alternative" concept in child placement decisions in all contexts.

President Johnson's crime commission nine years ago presented its most powerful argument for retention of a separate juvenile court in terms of an argument of less harm:

> The Commission does not conclude from its study of the juvenile court that the time has come to jettison the experiment and remand the disposition of children charged with crime to the criminal courts of the country. As trying as are the problems of the juvenile court, the problems of the criminal courts, particularly those of the lower courts that would fall heir to much of the juvenile court jurisdiction, are even graver. President's Commission on Law Enforcement and Administration of Justice, *The Challenge of Crime in a Free Society* 81 (1967).

The following standards and the commentary in support do not attempt to offer theoretical or ideological explanations. Nor do we necessarily adopt any one or more of the rationales offered here to the exclusion of the others. Sound social policies require a presumption that all persons under the juvenile court's maximum age jurisdiction should remain subject to the juvenile court's jurisdiction. Only extraordinary juveniles in extraordinary factual situations should be transferred to the criminal court and then only in accordance with procedures designed to accord maximum procedural protections to the juvenile and in compliance with precise and exacting behavioral standards.

Standards

PART I: JURISDICTION

1.1 Age limits.

A. The juvenile court should have jurisdiction in any proceeding against any person whose alleged conduct would constitute an offense on which a juvenile court adjudication could be based if at the time the offense is alleged to have occurred such person was not more than seventeen years of age.

B. No criminal court should have jurisdiction in any proceeding against any person whose alleged conduct would constitute an offense on which a juvenile court adjudication could be based if at the time the offense is alleged to have occurred such person was not more than fourteen years of age.

C. No criminal court should have jurisdiction in any proceeding against any person whose alleged conduct would constitute an offense on which a juvenile court adjudication could be based if at the time the offense is alleged to have occurred such person was fifteen, sixteen, or seventeen years of age, unless the juvenile court has waived its jurisdiction over that person.

1.2 Other limits.

A. No juvenile court disposition, however modified, resulting from a single transaction or episode, should exceed [thirty-six] months.

B. The juvenile court should retain jurisdiction to administer or modify its disposition of any person. The juvenile court should not have jurisdiction to adjudicate subsequent conduct of any person subject to such continuing jurisdiction if at the time the subsequent criminal offense is alleged to have occurred such person was more than seventeen years of age.

1.3 Limitations period.

No juvenile court adjudication or waiver decision should be based on an offense alleged to have occurred more than three years prior to the filing of a petition alleging such offense, unless such offense

9

would not be subject to a statute of limitations if committed by an adult. If the statute of limitations applicable to adult criminal proceedings for such offense is less than three years, such shorter period should apply to juvenile court criminal proceedings.

PART II: WAIVER

2.1 Time requirements.

 A. Within [two] court days of the filing of any petition alleging conduct which constitutes a class one or class two juvenile offense against a person who was fifteen, sixteen, or seventeen years of age when the alleged offense occurred, the clerk of the juvenile court should give the prosecuting attorney written notice of the possibility of waiver.

 B. Within [three] court days of the filing of any petition alleging conduct which constitutes a class one or class two juvenile offense against a person who was fifteen, sixteen, or seventeen years of age when the alleged offense occurred, the prosecuting attorney should give such person written notice, multilingual if appropriate, of the possibility of waiver.

 C. Within [seven] court days of the filing of any petition alleging conduct which constitutes a class one or class two juvenile offense against a person who was fifteen, sixteen, or seventeen years of age when the alleged offense occurred, the prosecuting attorney may request by written motion that the juvenile court waive its jurisdiction over the juvenile. The prosecuting attorney should deliver a signed, acknowledged copy of the waiver motion to the juvenile and counsel for the juvenile within [twenty-four] hours after the filing of such motion in the juvenile court.

 D. The juvenile court should initiate a hearing on waiver within [ten] court days of the filing of the waiver motion or, if the juvenile seeks to suspend this requirement, within a reasonable time thereafter.

 E. The juvenile court should issue a written decision setting forth its findings and the reasons therefor, including a statement of the evidence relied on in reaching the decision, within [ten] court days after conclusion of the waiver hearing.

 F. No waiver notice should be given, no waiver motion should be accepted for filing, no waiver hearing should be initiated, and no waiver decision should be issued relating to any juvenile court petition after commencement of any adjudicatory hearing relating to any transaction or episode alleged in that petition.

2.2 Necessary findings.

A. The juvenile court should waive its jurisdiction only upon finding:

    1. that probable cause exists to believe that the juvenile has committed the class one or class two juvenile offense alleged in the petition; and

    2. that by clear and convincing evidence the juvenile is not a proper person to be handled by the juvenile court.

B. A finding of probable cause to believe that a juvenile has committed a class one or class two juvenile offense should be based solely on evidence admissible in an adjudicatory hearing of the juvenile court.

C. A finding that a juvenile is not a proper person to be handled by the juvenile court must include determinations, by clear and convincing evidence, of:

    1. the seriousness of the alleged class one or class two juvenile offense;

    2. a prior record of adjudicated delinquency involving the infliction or threat of significant bodily injury, if the juvenile is alleged to have committed a class two juvenile offense;

    3. the likely inefficacy of the dispositions available to the juvenile court as demonstrated by previous dispositions of the juvenile; and

    4. the appropriateness of the services and dispositional alternatives available in the criminal justice system for dealing with the juvenile's problems and whether they are, in fact, available.

Expert opinion should be considered in assessing the likely efficacy of the dispositions available to the juvenile court. A finding that a juvenile is not a proper person to be handled by the juvenile court should be based solely on evidence admissible in a disposition hearing of the juvenile court and should be in writing, as provided in Standard 2.1 E.

D. A finding of probable cause to believe that a juvenile has committed a class one or class two juvenile offense may be substituted for a probable cause determination relating to that offense (or a lesser included offense) required in any subsequent juvenile court proceeding. Such a finding should not be substituted for any finding of probable cause required in any subsequent criminal proceeding.

2.3 The hearing.

A. The juvenile should be represented by counsel at the waiver hearing. The clerk of the juvenile court should give written notice to the juvenile, multilingual if appropriate, of this requirement at least [five] court days before commencement of the waiver hearing.

B. The juvenile court should appoint counsel to represent any juvenile unable to afford representation by counsel at the waiver hearing. The clerk of the juvenile court should give written notice to the juvenile, multilingual if appropriate, of this right at least [five] court days before commencement of the waiver hearing.

C. The juvenile court should pay the reasonable fees and expenses of an expert witness for the juvenile if the juvenile desires, but is unable to afford, the services of such an expert witness at the waiver hearing, unless the presiding officer determines that the expert witness is not necessary.

D. The juvenile should have access to all evidence available to the juvenile court which could be used either to support or contest the waiver motion.

E. The prosecuting attorney should bear the burden of proving that probable cause exists to believe that the juvenile has committed a class one or class two juvenile offense and that the juvenile is not a proper person to be handled by the juvenile court.

F. The juvenile may contest the waiver motion by challenging, or producing evidence tending to challenge, the evidence of the prosecuting attorney.

G. The juvenile may examine any person who prepared any report concerning the juvenile which is presented at the waiver hearing.

H. All evidence presented at the waiver hearing should be under oath and subject to cross-examination.

I. The juvenile may remain silent at the waiver hearing. No admission by the juvenile during the waiver hearing should be admissible to establish guilt or to impeach testimony in any subsequent proceeding, except a perjury proceeding.

J. The juvenile may disqualify the presiding officer at the waiver hearing from presiding at any subsequent criminal trial or juvenile court adjudicatory hearing relating to any transaction or episode alleged in the petition initiating juvenile court proceedings.

2.4 Appeal.

A. The juvenile or the prosecuting attorney may file an appeal of the waiver decision with the court authorized to hear appeals from final judgments of the juvenile court within [seven] court days of the decision of the juvenile court.

B. The appellate court should render its decision expeditiously, according the findings of the juvenile court the same weight given the findings of the highest court of general trial jurisdiction.

C. No criminal court should have jurisdiction in any proceeding relating to any transaction or episode alleged in the juvenile court petition as to which a waiver motion was made, against any person over whom the juvenile court has waived jurisdiction, until the time for filing an appeal from that determination has passed or, if such an appeal has been filed, until the final decision of the appellate court has been issued.

Standards with Commentary*

PART 1: JURISDICTION

1.1 Age limits.

A. The juvenile court should have jurisdiction in any proceeding against any person whose alleged conduct would constitute an offense on which a juvenile court adjudication could be based if at the time the offense is alleged to have occurred such person was not more than seventeen years of age.

Commentary

This standard addresses two major issues: the maximum age of juvenile court jurisdiction and the point at which the juvenile's age is relevant.

Standard 1.1 A. proposes that all accused persons seventeen and younger should be subject to juvenile court jurisdiction. The eighteenth birthday should define an adult for the purposes of court jurisdiction. The jurisdictional statutes of thirty-seven states agree. Nine states end juvenile court jurisdiction at the seventeenth birthday; four at the sixteenth. The eighteenth birthday signals the achievement of majority for many legal purposes. The twenty-sixth amendment to the United States Constitution establishes a constitutional right to vote in federal elections at that age. This near consensus among the states and the federal government argues compellingly that juvenile court jurisdiction should end at age eighteen.

Standard 1.1 A. bases jurisdiction on age at the time an act allegedly occurred that would constitute an offense on which a juvenile court adjudication could be based. One alternative is to look to age at the time that the juvenile court petition or the criminal court complaint, information, or indictment is filed. A majority of states base jurisdiction on a person's age at the time of the alleged conduct giving rise to juvenile court jurisdiction. See Iowa Code Ann. § 232.62 (1941); La. Rev. Stat. § 13.1569(3) (Supp. 1974); and W. Va. Code Ann. § 49-5-3 (Supp. 49, 1974). In some states the controlling

---

*On July 21, 1976, *Morales v. Turman*, 364 F. Supp. 166 (E.D. Tex. 1973), cited herein, was reversed on technical grounds by the Fifth Circuit Court of Appeals, *Morales et. al. v. Turman et. al.*, 535 F.2d 864.

factor is age when juvenile court proceedings are initiated. See Ky. Rev. Stat. Ann. § 208.020 (1969) and Mich. Comp. Laws Ann. § 712A.2 (Supp. 37, 1974).

The existence of a juvenile court reflects a social policy decision that the acts of juveniles ordinarily should not place them within the jurisdiction of the criminal court. To base juvenile court jurisdiction on any age other than that at the time of the alleged wrongful conduct would conflict with the fundamental concept that the acts of juveniles should receive different judicial treatment from those of adults.

A second argument for the time-of-conduct jurisdictional rule is the possibility that otherwise prosecutorial caprice could determine jurisdiction. Conduct that could be the basis for a juvenile court delinquency adjudication can usually also support a criminal prosecution. In a state where jurisdiction is based on age at the time of filing, a prosecutor can deny juvenile court jurisdiction simply by delaying the initiation of proceedings. Texas prosecutors have become notorious for this practice. See Note, "Trial of Juveniles as Adults," 21 *Baylor L. Rev.* 333 (1969) and Note, "Juvenile Due Process Texas-Style: Fruit of the Poisonous Tree Resweetened," 24 *Baylor L. Rev.* 71 (1972).

Standard 1.1 A.'s time-of-conduct age jurisdiction rule avoids a troublesome jurisdictional problem encountered in states (and the District of Columbia) that employ a two-part age jurisdiction standard; the individual must have been under a specified age at the time of the alleged conduct and must be under a second age at the time of adjudication. The gap between the time-of-conduct and time-of-adjudication limits is usually at least three years. Representative statutes include: Ga. Code Ann. § 24A–401(c)(2) (Supp. 9A, 1973); N.H. Rev. Stat. Ann. § 169:1 (Supp. 2, 1973); and Utah Code Ann. § 55–10–77 (1973).

The two-part age test produces anomalies. The customary situation involves an individual who meets the time-of-conduct age requirements but not the time-of-adjudication age. The juvenile can properly argue that the juvenile court lacks jurisdiction either to adjudicate the alleged conduct or to waive its jurisdiction. If the criminal court can have jurisdiction over the juvenile only after waiver, the juvenile can assert that no court has jurisdiction over the conduct alleged. Such an argument was accepted with little discussion in *Wilson v. Reagan,* 354 F.2d 45 (9th Cir. 1965).

Appellate courts strain to avoid the *Reagan* result. In *Kent v. United States,* 383 U.S. 541 (1965), the Supreme Court refused dismissal, recommending that the criminal court attempt to reconstruct

the waiver hearing. The commentary following Standards 2.4 A. and
B. suggests some defects of such a hearing.

Reagan and *Kent* concerned challenges to prior waiver hearings;
acceptance of those challenges and rejection of outright release made
reconstruction of the waiver hearings necessary. That outcome could
be avoided by rejecting the challenge to the prior hearing, as occurred
in *Mordecai v. United States*, 421 F.2d 1133 (D.C. Cir. 1969), and
Brown v. Cox, 481 F.2d 622 (4th Cir. 1973). Standard 1.1 A. avoids
this problem by basing age jurisdiction solely on time-of-conduct.

Assuming a successful appeal and a remand to the juvenile court,
an extended appeal from a waiver hearing can result in juvenile court
jurisdiction over persons beyond the court's customary age range.
Standard 2.4 attempts to lessen that possibility by requiring prompt
filing of appeals from waiver decisions and prompt resolution of
those appeals.

Jurisdiction based on time-of-conduct has the possible disadvantage
that delay in apprehension could produce a "juvenile" who is beyond
the customary age range of the juvenile court. Without further limitations on jurisdiction a thirty-year-old could be the subject of a juvenile
court adjudication. Standard 1.3 addresses that problem by establishing a three-year limitations period for the acts of juveniles.

**1.1 B. No criminal court should have jurisdiction in any proceeding
against any person whose alleged conduct would constitute an
offense on which a juvenile court adjudication could be based
if at the time the offense is alleged to have occurred such person was not more than fourteen years of age.**

Commentary

The juvenile court should have exclusive jurisdiction over persons
who were fourteen or younger at the time of the alleged criminal conduct. Standard 1.1 C. authorizes waiver of juvenile court jurisdiction
over persons who were fifteen, sixteen, or seventeen at the time of
the alleged conduct. This standard recognizes that any line between
adult and juvenile is necessarily arbitrary. Practical and political pres-
sures will sometimes require that persons otherwise subject to juvenile court jurisdiction be referred to the criminal court. Standards
1.1 A. and 1.1 C. create a rebuttable presumption that fifteen-,
sixteen-, and seventeen-year-olds should be treated as juveniles. This
standard reflects a determination that fourteen-year-olds are, or at
least should irrebuttably be presumed to be, juveniles for purposes
of court jurisdiction.

Minimum ages at which juveniles can appear in criminal courts vary widely. The minima result both from laws determining criminal responsibility and laws defining juvenile and criminal court jurisdiction. Prosecution of a mere infant is theoretically possible in Arizona. Ariz. Rev. Stat. Ann. § 13-135 (1956) presumes lack of criminal responsibility in children thirteen or under, but the prosecution can rebut the presumption with a showing that "at the time of committing the act charged against them they knew its wrongfulness." Under Ariz. R. Juv. P. 12, the juvenile court may waive its jurisdiction over any child subject to criminal prosecution. In Idaho and the District of Columbia, an alleged offender is subject to criminal prosecution only if he or she is eighteen or older at the time of trial. Idaho Code § 16-1806(1)(b) (Supp. 3, 1973) and D.C. Code Ann. § 16-2307(a)(3) (1973).

In thirteen states the lower limit of criminal jurisdiction is the sixteenth birthday: California, Hawaii, Idaho, Kansas, Montana, Nevada, New Jersey, New Mexico, North Dakota, Oregon, Rhode Island, Vermont, and Wisconsin. In nine and in twenty-five jurisdictions the minimum ages are fifteen and fourteen, respectively. The minimum is thirteen years of age in Illinois and twelve in Arkansas and Washington. Thus Standard 1.1 B. establishes a rule that presently exists only in a minority of the jurisdictions that allow waiver.

The realism of the minority rule adopted here is suggested by existing research on the incidence of waiver. Regardless of the permissible scope for waiver, its occurrence rarely extends beyond the last two years of juvenile court jurisdiction. Few fifteen-year-olds are waived to the criminal court. A recent study indicates that the juvenile courts in Nashville during a two-year period waived jurisdiction only over persons who were seventeen and thus in their last year of juvenile court eligibility. See Note, "Problem of Age and Jurisdiction in the Juvenile Court," 19 *Vand. L. Rev.* 833, 854 (1966). Similarly, a Houston survey of juveniles whose waiver was sought during a period in 1970 found that most were in the last two years. See Hays and Solway, "The Role of Psychological Evaluation in Certification of Juveniles for Trial as Adults," 9 *Houston L. Rev.* 709, 710 (1972).

A minimum age jurisdiction of fifteen years for the criminal court may enhance the juvenile court's public image. Exclusive jurisdiction over persons under fifteen evidences commitment to the proposition that juveniles are qualitatively different from adults and should be treated differently.

Standard 1.1 B. assumes that the criminal court does not hear appeals from the juvenile court. In jurisdictions in which that is not the case, Standard 1.1 B. should be modified to read "No criminal court should have *original* jurisdiction in any proceeding. . . ."

1.1 C. **No criminal court should have jurisdiction in any proceeding against any person whose alleged conduct would constitute an offense ȯn which a juvenile court adjudication could be based if at the time the offense is alleged to have occurred such person was fifteen, sixteen, or seventeen years of age, unless the juvenile court has waived its jurisdiction over that person.**

Commentary

Waiver by the juvenile court of its jurisdiction over certain persons is one mechanism by which persons otherwise subject to the juvenile court can be referred to the criminal court. There are other mechanisms. By "reverse certification," criminal courts can refer criminal defendants to the juvenile court for handling. The matter also can be settled by excluding from the juvenile court's jurisdiction persons accused of particular offenses regardless of age. The prosecutor then decides what court will have jurisdiction by deciding what criminal charge to allege.

This volume adopts a waiver approach in which the juvenile court judge, upon motion by the prosecutor, decides whether waiver of juvenile court jurisdiction is appropriate in the particular case.

Standard 1.1 C. prohibits criminal court jurisdiction over any person who was fifteen, sixteen, or seventeen at the time an act allegedly occurred that would constitute an offense on which a juvenile court adjudication could be based unless the juvenile court has waived its jurisdiction over such person.

The standard recognizes that the eighteenth birthday is an arbitrary point at which to draw the line between juveniles and adults. Standard 1.1 C. allows a wide two-year age range in which waiver is possible. At the same time, a fundamental premise of this volume is that the vast majority of juveniles should be handled by the juvenile court. Later standards in this volume establish a rigorous test that must be met before any person otherwise within the juvenile court's jurisdiction can properly be waived to the criminal court.

The standards recognize that arguments will be made as to why certain individuals are not proper persons to be handled by the juvenile court. Among those arguments will be: the seriousness of the alleged offense; public demands for harsher treatment of juvenile offenders; the age or prior criminal record of the individual; or the demonstrated inefficacy of juvenile court programs. By allowing a liberal age range but a strict test for waiver's appropriateness, this volume offers the view that the clearly dangerous juvenile should be waived, even if only fifteen, but no one else.

Only New York bars waiver. N.Y. Family Ct. Act § 713 (McKinney 1962) grants "exclusive original jurisdiction" to the state's juvenile courts. New York law provides no mechanism to relieve the juvenile court of the task of handling persons within the court's age jurisdiction. This seemingly brave experiment commits the state to attempt to treat as juveniles all those statutorily defined as juveniles.

A lack of flexibility appears to be the major flaw in New York's Family Court Act. The New York legislature lowered the maximum age for court jurisdiction to fifteen—see N.Y. Family Ct. Act § 712(a) (McKinney Supp. 29A, 1973)—and the sixteen- or seventeen-year-old is therefore never eligible for juvenile court treatment.

Standard 1.1 C. manifests an intention to define juvenile court jurisdiction broadly. The juvenile court can subsequently waive those juveniles for whom juvenile court jurisdiction is found inappropriate. Without some ability to select, the juvenile court must misallocate its efforts and limited resources on juveniles who appear unlikely to benefit from juvenile court programs. Failure to deal constructively with the most troublesome juveniles might produce legislative pressure, as in New York, to lower the maximum age for juvenile court jurisdiction. Contraction of jurisdiction would force many persons into the criminal courts who might benefit from the special handling of the juvenile court. A flexible case-by-case waiver scheme is far preferable to the New York approach.

Standard 1.1 C. provides that the juvenile court, rather than a criminal court, should be the setting for the waiver decision. The criminal court may assert jurisdiction only after the juvenile court waives. This approach follows the example of the Model Penal Code § 4.10(1) (Proposed Official Draft 1962).

The alternative to juvenile court decision-making power is reverse certification, in which the juvenile first appears before a criminal court. The criminal court judge decides whether to retain jurisdiction or to certify the case to the juvenile court. California had such a system until the California legislature amended Cal. Welf. & Inst'ns Code § 604 in 1971. Only Arkansas and Vermont currently employ reverse certification exclusively. See Ark. Stat. § 45–241 (1964), and Vt. Stat. Ann. tit. 33, § 635(b) (Supp. 9, 1974).

A principal argument against reverse certification is that the juvenile court ought to, and has special competence to, interpret the laws regulating its own jurisdiction. Granting the criminal court primary responsibility for the decision invites abuse. The juvenile court judge is more aware of the juvenile court's capacities and limitations, and he or she should make the waiver decision.

Reverse certification is also incompatible with the juvenile court's conceptual underpinnings. The court's very existence is premised on the view that the special characteristics of juveniles require that they receive different judicial treatment than adults. Any waiver mechanism consistent with that view must institutionalize a presumption in favor of juvenile court jurisdiction. Reverse certification institutionalizes the opposite presumption: that juveniles are subject to the criminal court's jurisdiction unless special steps are taken.

Standard 1.1 C. assumes that the criminal court does not hear appeals from the juvenile court. In jurisdictions in which that assumption is unfounded, Standard 1.1 C. should be modified to read "No criminal court should have *original* jurisdiction in any proceeding. . . ."

1.2 Other limits.

A. No juvenile court disposition, however modified, resulting from a single transaction or episode, should exceed [thirty-six] months.

Commentary

Standard 1.2 A. places a maximum [three-year] limit on any juvenile court disposition resulting from a single episode or transaction.

One of the fundamental modern criticisms of the juvenile court has been that it subjects juveniles to longer and harsher interventions in their lives than are experienced by adults accused of the same unlawful acts. Gerald Gault, the principal of *In Re Gault*, 387 U.S. 1 (1967), was found to have violated an Arizona statute prohibiting "vulgar, abusive or obscene language . . . in the presence or hearing of any woman or child. . . ." Ariz. Rev. Stat. Ann. § 13–377 (1956). An adult convicted of that offense could be imprisoned for no more than sixty days. Gerald Gault was committed to the State Industrial School until he reached majority at age twenty-one, unless sooner discharged.

Juvenile courts in Kansas and Rhode Island may retain dispositional jurisdiction over juveniles until the twenty-first birthday, even if the juvenile was only twelve or thirteen when the disposition was ordered. See Kan. Stat. Ann. § 38–806(b) (Supp. 3, 1973) and R.I. Gen. Laws Ann. § 14–1–6 (1956). In forty-six states and the District of Columbia, juvenile courts retain authority over persons previously adjudicated after the maximum age for initial jurisdiction has passed. The court customarily retains jurisdiction to administer its dispositions until the juvenile's twenty-first birthday. See Mont. Rev. Codes Ann. § 10-1206(1) (Supp. vol. 1, pt. 2, 1974) and Okla. Stat. Ann. ch. 10, § 1102 (Supp. 10, 1974).

Hawaii, Massachusetts, South Dakota, Vermont, and West Virginia do not permit retained jurisdiction to administer dispositions beyond the maximum adjudicatory age jurisdiction of the juvenile court. Those states initially deny the court power to adjudicate or to supervise a disposition of any person over seventeen. See Hawaii Rev. Stat. §§ 571-11(1), 571-13 (Supp. 7, 1973); Mass. Gen. Laws Ann. ch. 119, § 68 (Supp. 18, 1974); S.D. Compiled Laws Ann. §§ 26-8-1(3), 26-8-48, 26-1-1 (Supp. 9, 1974); Vt. Stat. Ann. tit. 33, §§ 633(a), 632(a)(1), 634, tit. 1, § 173 (Supp. 1, 1974); and W. Va. Code Ann. §§ 49-5-2, 49-2-2 (Supp. 14, 1974). Those statutory provisions reflect a view that a person who is not a juvenile for adjudicatory purposes should not be a juvenile for dispositional purposes.

There are circumstances in which the court should have authority over persons beyond the maximum age for initial adjudication. Apprehension may occur shortly before the eighteenth birthday. If dispositional authority beyond the eighteenth birthday is lacking, powerful incentive either to waive juvenile court jurisdiction or not to invoke the juvenile court process at all will result.

Denial of dispositional jurisdiction beyond the court's maximum adjudicatory age limit would result in several anomalies. For instance, a juvenile could allegedly commit a criminal act on his or her seventeenth birthday. If a rigorous test for the propriety of waiver exists in the jurisdiction, as this volume recommends, the juvenile might not be waivable and in one month would be beyond the authority of any court. Similarly, the concept of a statute of limitations such as that suggested in Standard 1.3 is compatible only with extended dispositional jurisdiction. A three-year limitations period in a state having an eighteenth birthday maximum age jurisdiction would actually be the lesser of three years or the period of time remaining before the eighteenth birthday.

Abolition of retained jurisdiction would create pressure to transfer for criminal prosecution any older juvenile accused of serious criminal conduct. Waiver would be attractive because the juvenile court could enforce its disposition only for a short period, while the criminal court would have greater dispositional authority. A fundamental premise of this volume is that the vast majority of persons within the juvenile court's age jurisdiction who are alleged to have committed criminal acts should be handled by the juvenile court. To deny juvenile court handling because there is not sufficient time to provide it is inconsistent with that premise.

When waiver is not possible because the alleged conduct occurred before the juvenile's fifteenth birthday or, as in New York, waiver is simply not authorized, the argument for extending jurisdiction is different. Without retained dispositional jurisdiction there would be a strong inducement to release a juvenile apprehended at seventeen for a crime committed at fourteen. The limited duration of juvenile court jurisdiction could make adjudication and short-term disposition of the juvenile a misallocation of the court's limited resources.

Most states permit retained dispositional jurisdiction. The most common approach allows the juvenile court to impose its disposition until the juvenile reaches a certain age, usually from one to four years beyond the maximum age for adjudication. This is the system that Gerald Gault experienced and subjects younger juveniles to dispositional jurisdiction for very long periods.

A few states, including Connecticut, New York, and Pennsylvania, allow retention of dispositional jurisdiction for a specified period of years following adjudication. Jurisdiction to impose a disposition lasts two years in Connecticut and the juvenile court may renew the jurisdiction for another two-year period. See Conn. Gen. Stat. Ann. § 17-69 (Supp. 10, 1974). New York authorizes dispositional jurisdiction for three years after adjudication. See N.Y. Family Ct. Act § 758 (McKinney Supp. 29A, 1973). Pennsylvania law also authorizes a three-year dispositional period and, as in Connecticut, grants the juvenile court power to renew the period. See Pa. Stat. Ann. tit. 11, § 50-323 (Supp. 11, 1974). However, the court may retain dispositional jurisdiction past the maximum age for adjudication only if the juvenile was apprehended after reaching a specified age: thirteen in New York; twelve in Connecticut and Pennsylvania. This fixed term of years approach is preferable to its more popular alternative. Fixed duration dispositional authority also lessens the disparity between the maximum periods of court control faced by juveniles and adults alleged to have committed certain offenses.

1.2 B. The juvenile court should retain jurisdiction to administer or modify its disposition of any person. The juvenile court should not have jurisdiction to adjudicate subsequent conduct of any person subject to such continuing jurisdiction if at the time the subsequent criminal offense is alleged to have occurred such person was more than seventeen years of age.

Commentary

Standard 1.2 B. bars adjudications based on conduct occurring during the extended period of dispositional jurisdiction of persons not otherwise within the court's age jurisdiction. Standard 1.1 A. implicitly achieves the same result. However, an unequivocal declaration was considered appropriate. Such a provision contradicts statutes like Mich. Comp. Laws Ann. § 712A.22 (Supp. 37, 1974) that permit adjudication of previously adjudicated and disposed seventeen- and eighteen-year-olds even though the maximum age for initial juvenile court jurisdiction is sixteen. Michigan limits such permissible subsequent adjudications to allegations of noncriminal conduct. Thus, section 712A.22 subjects an eighteen-year-old whom the juvenile court has adjudicated and disposed to a further adjudication if the juvenile repeatedly disobeys the commands of his or her parents.

The prohibition on new adjudications should not bar modifications of disposition during the period of extended jurisdiction. Such a bar would unduly restrict the juvenile court's dispositional options. A juvenile's conduct while subject to a juvenile court disposition is material to decisions to modify that disposition. There will be occasions when distinguishing between a proper modification of a disposition and an improper imposition of what is in substance an additional disposition without an additional adjudication will be difficult. The bases for modifying dispositional decisions are discussed in the *Dispositions* volume. *Dispositions* Standard 5.4 provides that when a juvenile fails to comply with a dispositional order and a warning is insufficient to induce compliance, the court may modify conditions or impose the next most severe disposition, but may not extend its duration. Thus probation (community supervision) could be revoked and a custodial disposition in a nonsecure residence substituted for the remainder of the dispositional term if a warning or changed conditions of probation would be ineffective.

1.3 Limitations period.

No juvenile court adjudication or waiver decision should be based on an offense alleged to have occurred more than three years prior to the filing of a petition alleging such offense, unless such offense would not be subject to a statute of limitations if committed by an adult. If the statute of limitations applicable to adult criminal proceedings for such offense is less than three years, such shorter period should apply to juvenile court criminal proceedings.

Commentary

Standard 1.3 establishes a three-year statute of limitations for juvenile court adjudications in most cases. Standard 1.3 rejects the two most common existing limitations approaches in juvenile courts: incorporation of statutes limiting criminal prosecutions, and application of equitable principles of limitation. This standard incorporates adult statutes of limitations only to the extent that they establish limitation periods shorter than three years or provide no limitations period for specified serious criminal offenses.

Standards 1.1 A., 1.2 A., and 1.3 combine to authorize the juvenile court to maintain jurisdiction over a juvenile until age twenty-four. Standard 1.1 A. gives the court jurisdiction over persons under eighteen at the time-of-conduct. Standard 1.3 creates a three-year limitations period for most offenses. The juvenile a day short of age eighteen at the time-of-conduct could be two days short of twenty-one when the petition is filed. Disregarding the time required for adjudication, the three-year maximum disposition authorized by Standard 1.2 A. would permit the court to retain jurisdiction over that individual until almost his or her twenty-fourth birthday.

New Jersey's juvenile courts have been among the leaders in applying criminal statutes of limitations to juvenile court proceedings. In *State in the Interest of B.H.*, 270 A.2d 72 (N.J. 1970), a juvenile and domestic relations court held that the one-year limit on prosecutions under the Disorderly Persons Act restricted the filing of juvenile petitions as well:

> The lapse of the statutory period for prosecution is not a procedural defense; it is substantive and jurisdictional. . . . It would indeed be anomalous to award juveniles an ever-expanding shield of procedural protection, but deny them the right to plead a substantive defense. *Id.* at 74.

Dictum in *State in the Interest of K.V.N.*, 271 A.2d 921 (N.J. 1970), endorses this view, as does Standard 1.3.

Periods of limitation frequently vary by offense. New Jersey employs a one-year limit for disorderly conduct but five years for armed robbery or rape.

A three-year limitations period has the advantages of certainty and predictability. The certainty of the three-year limit is preferable to the frequently arbitrary differences between limitations periods for different offenses.

The view of delinquency summarized in E. Schur's *Radical Nonintervention—Rethinking the Delinquency Problem* (1973) holds that most juveniles will outgrow propensities for antisocial acts if left alone. The 1973 Report of the National Advisory Commission on Criminal Justice Standards and Goals largely supported that view. See National Advisory Commission on Criminal Justice Standards and Goals, *A National Strategy to Reduce Crime* 109 (1973). For those offenses subject to the three-year limit, Standard 1.3 embodies the view that acts that occurred more than three years before the filing of a petition are not valid indicators of a juvenile's social adjustment, notwithstanding that the adult limitations period exceeds three years.

The juvenile should, however, receive the benefit of any adult limitations period shorter than three years. Being a juvenile should not justify intervention that adults who have engaged in similar criminal conduct do not experience. The argument in support of incorporation by reference of shorter adult limitations periods is similar to that in support of the maximum three-year dispositional jurisdiction of Standard 1.2 A.

Some juvenile courts have applied equitable concepts to limitations problems. The Oklahoma Court of Criminal Appeals in *Sorrels v. Steele*, 506 P.2d 942 (Okla. 1973), voided a delinquency finding, in part for staleness reasons:

> It should be apparent that one isolated incident removed in point of time by some thirty-one months is far too remote to have any possible bearing on the current conduct of a fourteen-year-old girl, much less to be considered as part of a basis for adjudicating her a delinquent. *Id.* at 944.

Standard 1.3 permits the flexibility of the equitable limitations approach, and implements the "least intrusive alternative" policy of these standards.

Standard 1.3 omits from the statute of limitations the customary list of circumstances that suspend the limitation period. Flight from the jurisdiction or concealment of criminal conduct will not toll the statute. Such exceptions have no place in a juvenile court statute of limitations. The arguments in support of a three-year limitations period for most juvenile offenses apply equally even if the alleged criminal conduct has been concealed or the juvenile has been outside the jurisdiction.

Standard 1.3 incorporates by reference the provisions of criminal law statutes of limitations that except certain offenses, usually murder, rape, and other serious criminal acts. The seriousness of those particular criminal acts, which gives rise to the criminal court provisions, applies equally in the juvenile court. The juvenile accused of an excepted offense regarding which the general limitations period has run out will not necessarily be subject to waiver. If the alleged conduct occurred before the juvenile's fifteenth birthday, waiver will not be possible in any event. If the alleged conduct occurred while the juvenile was fifteen, sixteen, or seventeen, the general standards for waiver will apply.

PART II: WAIVER

2.1 Time requirements.
A. Within [two] court days of the filing of any petition alleging conduct which constitutes a class one or class two juvenile offense against a person who was fifteen, sixteen, or seventeen years of age when the alleged offense occurred, the clerk of the juvenile court should give the prosecuting attorney written notice of the possibility of waiver.

Commentary

Standard 2.1 A. requires the clerk of the juvenile court to give prompt written notice to the prosecuting attorney of the filing of petitions against fifteen-, sixteen-, and seventeen-year-olds with class one or class two juvenile offenses. The recommended time requirement has been bracketed to indicate that it is not mandatory, since calendar backlogs, resources, and other circumstances may vary significantly among jurisdictions. This is consistent with the policy adopted throughout the revised versions of the standards to bracket all such numerical limitations (see Preface).

Standards 2.1 B. through 2.1 E. similarly require prompt consideration and resolution of waiver motions. Delay can have an adverse impact on the juvenile regardless of the outcome of the juvenile court proceeding. If the petition is dismissed, for whatever reason, intervention in the juvenile's life should be as short and unobtrusive as possible. If the petition results in a delinquency adjudication, the juvenile should be spared unnecessary delay in the imposition of a disposition. The disposition should begin promptly. The adverse effects of juvenile court processing should be minimized.

The problems of delay are multiplied during the waiver process. The subject of an unresolved waiver proceeding is in limbo. Neither the juvenile court nor the criminal court can act upon the criminal charges until the waiver motion is decided.

Notice to the prosecuting attorney of the possibility of waiver is necessary only when the petition alleges conduct which would constitute a class one or class two juvenile offense. Standard 2.2 A. prohibits waiver unless the juvenile court finds probable cause to believe that the juvenile committed a class one or class two juvenile offense. The term "class one juvenile offense" is defined in the

Juvenile Delinquency and Sanctions volume as those criminal offenses for which the maximum sentence for adults would be death or imprisonment for life or a term in excess of twenty years. A "class two juvenile offense" is one for which an adult could be imprisoned for a term in excess of five but not more than twenty years.

2.1 B. Within [three] court days of the filing of any petition alleging conduct which constitutes a class one or class two juvenile offense against a person who was fifteen, sixteen, or seventeen years of age when the alleged offense occurred, the prosecuting attorney should give such person written notice, multilingual if appropriate, of the possibility of waiver.

Commentary

Standard 2.1 B. requires the prosecuting attorney to give prompt consideration to the possibility of waiver proceedings against fifteen-, sixteen-, and seventeen-year-olds accused of class one or class two juvenile offenses. For reasons discussed in the commentary following Standard 2.1 C., the prosecuting attorney should have exclusive authority to initiate waiver proceedings.

The notice must be given within [three] court days of the filing of the petition alleging conduct that would constitute a class one or class two juvenile offense. Failure to give timely notice would be a fatal defect to any waiver proceeding.

The prosecuting attorney will be compelled to determine within [three] court days whether waiver is appropriate in each case. If timely notice is not given, the juvenile court can proceed to consider the petition on the merits. If the notice is given, the juvenile will be informed early that he or she may be waived to the criminal court.

Some prosecutorial offices might respond to Standard 2.1 B. by giving notice in every case in which waiver is possible. Although such a procedure would partially frustrate the objectives of the notice requirement, the juvenile would be put on notice of the possibility of waiver in the case. Other prosecutorial offices might comply with the spirit of 2.1 B. and signal their intention not to seek waiver by not giving notice. In those offices which establish a standard notice procedure, Standard 2.1 C., which requires filing of the waiver motion within [seven] court days of the filing of the juvenile court petition, minimizes the uncertainty which the juvenile faces.

Multilingual notices should be given when the language primarily spoken by the juvenile is not English.

2.1 C. Within [seven] court days of the filing of any petition alleging conduct which constitutes a class one or class two juvenile offense against a person who was fifteen, sixteen, or seventeen years of age when the alleged offense occurred, the prosecuting attorney may request by written motion that the juvenile court waive its jurisdiction over the juvenile. The prosecuting attorney should deliver a signed, acknowledged copy of the waiver motion to the juvenile and counsel for the juvenile within [twenty-four] hours after the filing of such motion in the juvenile court.

Commentary

Standard 2.1 C. gives the prosecuting attorney sole authority to determine which juveniles will not be the subjects of waiver motions. A decision not to seek waiver can be indicated definitively by not filing a waiver motion within [seven] court days of the filing of the juvenile court petition. The prosecuting attorney may initiate, but not decide, waiver proceedings.

Prosecutorial authority to initiate, but not decide, waiver diverges from present practice in most states. See Minn. Stat. Ann. § 260.125(1) (1971) for one of the few exceptions.

Prosecuting attorneys customarily possess authority to waive juvenile jurisdiction in either of two ways. Some juvenile courts have concurrent jurisdiction with the criminal courts. See, *e.g.*, Wyo. Stat. Ann. § 14-115.4(c) (Supp. 5, 1973), and *Fugate v. Ponin*, 91 N.W.2d 240 (Neb. 1958). Prosecuting attorneys in those jurisdictions determine court jurisdiction by deciding whether to file a petition in juvenile court or a complaint in criminal court.

Prosecuting attorneys in some jurisdictions can determine court jurisdiction by alleging certain criminal acts. Some juvenile courts lack jurisdiction over certain crimes. Ten states and the District of Columbia have such provisions. See, *e.g.*, Colo. Rev. Stat. Ann. § 22-1-3(17) (1963), Del. Code Ann. tit. 10, § 957 (1953), Ind. Code § 31-5-7-4(1) (1973), and D.C. Code Ann. § 16-2301(3) (1973). Such laws permit the prosecuting attorney to select a forum by selecting a charge. District of Columbia criminal courts may retain jurisdiction to try the juvenile for a lesser included offense even if the alleged lesser included offense by itself would not have warranted criminal court jurisdiction. Prosecuting attorneys can abuse such a system by charging a juvenile with conduct over which the juvenile court lacks jurisdiction. After juvenile court jurisdiction has been avoided, the charge can be reduced to a crime more susceptible of proof. Such license to charge capriciously grants the prosecutor unfettered discretion to determine court jurisdiction over juveniles.

Mr. Justice Douglas, dissenting from denial of a petition for certiorari in *United States v. Bland*, 412 U.S. 909 (1973), presented a forceful argument against prosecutorial authority to determine juvenile court jurisdiction. Bland, a sixteen-year-old District of Columbia resident, was charged with armed robbery. The District of Columbia juvenile courts lack jurisdiction over armed robbery. The district court upheld Bland's constitutional objections to unreviewable prosecutorial discretion to charge Bland with an offense triable only in the criminal courts. 330 F. Supp. 34 (D.C.D.C. 1970). The court of appeals reversed. 472 F.2d 1329 (D.C. Cir. 1972). Bland's petition for certiorari to the United States Supreme Court was denied.

Justice Douglas argued against prosecutorial discretion to determine court jurisdiction over juveniles:

> A juvenile or "child" is placed in a more protected position than an adult. . . . In that category he is theoretically subject to rehabilitative treatment. Can he, on the whim or caprice of a prosecutor, be put in the class of run-of-the-mill criminal defendants, without any hearing, without any chance to be heard, without an opportunity to rebut the evidence against him, without a chance of showing that he is being given an invidiously different treatment from others in his group? 412 U.S. 909 at 911.

This potential for arbitrary and unequal treatment of juveniles is aggravated by the absence of review of prosecutorial decisions. This is the "barricade behind which the prosecutor operates." *Id.*

Justice Douglas' policy argument in *Bland* is persuasive whatever its present constitutional force. The very existence of juvenile courts should evidence a policy decision that juveniles should be subject to juvenile court jurisdiction unless a considered decision is made that criminal court jurisdiction is appropriate in the given case. This volume has adopted a strong presumption in favor of juvenile court jurisdiction. The presumption can properly be overcome only in a trial-type, due process proceeding in which the decision-making process is visible, based on identifiable and credible information and subject to review. The power of the prosecutor to make unreviewable waiver decisions at a low level of visibility invites capricious decisions.

Standard 2.1 C. strikes a balance between unlimited prosecutorial authority to waive juvenile court jurisdiction and no authority at all. Standard 2.1 C. grants the prosecuting attorney discretion to bar waiver; the juvenile court may consider waiver only upon the prosecutor's motion. The prosecuting attorney, often an elected official, may weigh political considerations in deciding whether to seek waiver and thereby express public outrage at a particularly serious offense. As the official who can properly take public sentiments into account, the prosecutor can partially insulate the juvenile court judge, who cannot properly consider such matters, from public pressure. The juvenile court judge must base the waiver decision on the findings required by Standard 2.2 A., thus providing judicial review of the prosecutor's actions.

It could be argued that Standard 2.1 C. grants too much authority to the prosecuting attorney; the juvenile court should be able to consider waiver on its own motion and should not be bound by the prosecutor's decision not to seek waiver. Several state legislatures have accepted this reasoning. Virginia amended its waiver statute in 1973 to replace prosecutorial discretion to waive with a hearing procedure that may be initiated by either the prosecuting attorney or the juvenile court judge. Va. Code Ann. § 16.1-176 (Supp. 4, 1974).

Virginia's procedure compromises the integrity of the court. The court should assume a passive stance, deciding in an impartial fashion only those questions necessary for resolution of the case before it. Raising issues sua sponte is undesirable for it shifts the court from a passive to an active role. The impartiality of the court's resolution of an issue raised on its own motion is inherently suspect. The court must be concerned with both the fact and the appearance of fairness and impartiality. The court's behavior will appear less than even-handed to the juvenile whose treatment as a juvenile is first questioned by the juvenile court judge. Juvenile court judges should rule on waiver but their judicial status should prevent their initiating the subject.

A third approach to deciding jurisdiction over juveniles is to prohibit waiver and thereby deny discretion to both the juvenile court judge and the prosecuting attorney, as in New York. Some objections to that approach are discussed in the commentary following Standard 1.2 C.

2.1 D.   The juvenile court should initiate a hearing on waiver within [ten] court days of the filing of the waiver motion or, if the juvenile seeks to suspend this requirement, within a reasonable time thereafter.

Commentary

Standard 2.1 D. requires the juvenile court to begin a waiver hearing within [ten] court days after the waiver motion is filed. Waiver of jurisdiction must be premised on the findings required by Standard 2.2 A. based on evidence presented at an adversary hearing.

The United States Supreme Court approved a similar hearing requirement for the District of Columbia in *Kent v. United States*, 383 U.S. 541 (1966). Kent confessed to involvement in the robbery and rape of a District of Columbia resident. The juvenile court waived jurisdiction over him without a hearing and without published reasons. After extensive but unsuccessful efforts to appeal the waiver decision, Kent was convicted of robbery, but not rape. The judgment was affirmed by the District of Columbia Court of Appeals. 343 F.2d 247 (D.C. Cir. 1964).

The Supreme Court disapproved waiver without a hearing:

> [C]onsidering particularly that decision as to waiver of jurisdiction and transfer of the matter to the District Court was potentially as important to petitioner as the difference between five years' confinement and a death sentence, we conclude that, as a condition to a valid waiver order, petitioner was entitled to a hearing, . . . and to a statement of reasons for the juvenile court's decision. We believe that this result is required by the statute read in the context of constitutional principles relating to due process and the assistance of counsel. 383 U.S. 541 at 557.

The sentence last quoted has plagued attempts to assess *Kent's* significance. Is a waiver hearing necessary because of "constitutional principles" or because of the particular District of Columbia statute? Does procedural due process require that a hearing precede resolution?

The importance of the constitutional question should not be overemphasized. Even if *Kent* concerned only statutory construction, the arguments for a hearing on the waiver issue would remain strong, given the potential prejudice to the juvenile in denying juvenile court jurisdiction without a hearing and opportunity to object. Disposition by a court of a critically important motion without hearing arguments or receiving evidence lacks fundamental fairness.

An adversary hearing is the best method for judicial resolution of the waiver issue. An overwhelming majority of state legislatures agree. For the minority view see, *e.g.*, Ala. Code tit. 13, § 364 (1959) and Miss. Code Ann. § 43-21-31 (1972). Faced with similar statutory provisions (most of which have now been redrafted), a number of state courts have found waiver hearings to be required constitutionally.

The Supreme Court of Indiana held "in accordance with *Kent*" that the appellant had a right to a full juvenile court hearing prior to waiver. *Summers v. State*, 230 N.E.2d 320, 325 (Ind. 1967). Oregon's highest court found "that the intent of the United States Supreme Court . . . is that the due process clause of the Constitution of the United States requires states to accord a hearing before a juvenile can be remanded to the adult criminal process." *Bouge v. Reed*, 459 P.2d 869, 870 (Ore. 1969). See also *In re Harris*, 434 P.2d 615 (Cal. 1967); *Smith v. Commonwealth*, 412 S.W.2d 256 (Ky. 1967); and *Jefferson v. State*, 442 S.W.2d 6 (Mo. 1969).

Some courts have disagreed. The Supreme Court of Appeals of Virginia did so in *Cradle v. Peyton*, 156 S.E.2d 874 (Va. 1967). However, most state courts have emphasized the constitutional foundations of *Kent*. "Although our decision turned upon the language of the statute, we emphasized the necessity that 'the basic requirements of due process and fairness' be satisfied in such proceedings." *In re Gault*, 387 U.S. 1, 12 (1967).

One commentator has remarked that "[a]fter a careful reading of *Kent* and *Gault*, a question as to the constitutional status of the holdings in the former case would seem pure rhetoric." Schornhorst, "The Waiver of Juvenile Court Jurisdiction: *Kent* Revisited," 43 *Ind. L.J.* 583, 585 (1968). This opinion is based on the significance of the waiver decision and the consequent need for procedural safeguards, steps in analysis which "bristle with constitutional indicia." *Id.* at 586.

Standard 2.1 D. conforms to prevailing constitutional opinion regarding waiver hearings. If that view is subsequently rejected as a matter of constitutional law, the policy reasons in support of a hearing requirement remain strong.

2.1 E. The juvenile court should issue a written decision setting forth its findings and the reasons therefor, including a statement of the evidence relied on in reaching the decision, within [ten] court days after conclusion of the waiver hearing.

Commentary

Standard 2.1 E. requires the juvenile court to issue a written decision on the waiver motion setting forth its findings and the reasons therefor within [ten] court days after conclusion of the waiver hearing.

Kent requires not only a hearing but also that the juvenile court state the reasons for its decision. *Kent v. United States*, 383 U.S. 541, 557 (1966). Indiana's highest court explicitly accorded both of these holdings full constitutional authority in *Summers v. State*, 230 N.E.2d 320 (Ind. 1967).

Kent's statement of reasons requirement has been adopted in a number of jurisdictions. The state courts, exercising their powers to promulgate rules of court, have been the prime movers. See, *e.g.*, Ohio R. Juv. P. 30(E), Wash. Juv. Ct. R. 6.4, and Fla. Juv. R. 8.100(c).

The importance of written decisions cannot be overstated. Written decisions discourage slipshod decision making in the particular case and in the juvenile process generally. More care may be exercised if the juvenile court judge realizes that decisions can be scrutinized. Statements of findings and reasoning in particular cases may benefit other judges in similar proceedings. Written decisions will narrow the range of questions on which reasonable judges may disagree and focus attention on those questions. Reasoned elaboration of the law will be promoted.

The argument for written decisions would remain strong even if the intellectual rigor of waiver decisions was guaranteed and every reasonably disputable question was removed from the waiver statute. The appearance of accountability created by explained decisions is beneficial to the juvenile court. A decision unsupported by reasons or based on reasons unsupported by evidence appears arbitrary, regardless of its actual character.

2.1 F. No waiver notice should be given, no waiver motion should be accepted for filing, no waiver hearing should be initiated, and no waiver decision should be issued relating to any juvenile court petition after commencement of any adjudicatory hearing relating to any transaction or episode alleged in that petition.

Commentary

Standard 2.1 F. prohibits consideration of waiver after adjudicatory proceedings have begun. Any other approach would be incompatible with *Breed v. Jones*, 421 U.S. 519 (1975), which held that jeopardy attaches for purposes of double jeopardy when the juvenile court, as the trier of fact, begins to hear evidence.

A juvenile court petition was filed against Gary Steven Jones, then seventeen, alleging that he had committed acts which if committed by an adult would constitute robbery. The juvenile court, after taking evidence from two prosecution witnesses and the juvenile, found that the allegations were true. Three weeks later the juvenile court determined that Jones was unsuitable for treatment as a juvenile and waived jurisdiction. Jones was subsequently convicted in criminal court of armed robbery in the first degree.

After a number of unsuccessful appeals from the waiver decision on double jeopardy grounds, Jones persuaded the Circuit Court of Appeals for the Ninth Circuit that the double jeopardy clause of the fifth amendment to the United States Constitution "is fully applicable to juvenile court proceedings." 497 F.2d 1160, 1165 (9th Cir. 1974). The Supreme Court granted certiorari to resolve the conflict on that question among federal courts of appeals and state supreme courts.

With the exception of *McKeiver v. Pennsylvania*, 403 U.S. 528 (1971), which held that jury trials are not required in juvenile court adjudicatory proceedings, the trend of recent Supreme Court decisions on juvenile court issues has been to apply criminal court procedural protections to juvenile court proceedings. *Breed v. Jones* is in line with that policy. On the applicability to juvenile court proceedings of the double jeopardy clause, the Supreme Court concluded:

> We believe it is simply too late in the day to conclude, as did the District Court in this case, that a juvenile is not put in jeopardy at a proceeding whose object is to determine whether he had committed acts that violate a criminal law and whose potential consequences include both the stigma inherent in such a determination and the deprivation of liberty for many years. *Breed v. Jones*, 421 U.S. at 529.

Breed v. Jones laid to rest any remaining doubts as to the applicability of the double jeopardy clause to juvenile court proceedings. It would appear that the *Gault* decision, when read in conjunction with the Court's subsequent decision in *Benton v. Maryland*, 395 U.S. 784 (1969), which applied the double jeopardy clause of the fifth amendment to state criminal proceedings, made *Breed v. Jones* inevitable.

Moquin v. State, 140 A.2d 914 (Md. 1958), epitomizes state court opinions concerning double jeopardy claims raised by juveniles before *Gault*, *Benton*, and *Breed v. Jones*:

> . . . [T]he rule of double jeopardy is applicable only when the first prosecution involves a trial before a criminal court or at least a court empowered to impose punishment by way of fine, imprisonment or otherwise as a deterrent to the commission of crime. The question to be decided is whether the hearing before the Juvenile Court of Montgomery County subjected the defendant to the risk of these penalties. We answer this question in the negative. 140 A.2d at 916.

The Maryland Court of Appeals focused on a rehabilitative rationale for the juvenile court, rather than on the impact of an adjudication on the juvenile:

> The juvenile act does not contemplate the punishment of children where they are found to be delinquent. The act contemplates an attempt to correct and rehabilitate. . . . [W]hile the act recognizes that there will be cases where hospital care or commitment to a juvenile training school or other institution may be necessary, this is all directed to the rehabilitation of the child concerned rather than punishment for any delinquent conduct. *Id.* at 916-17.

The pre-*Breed* state legislatures were only slightly more willing to extend protection against double jeopardy to juveniles than were the state courts. New Mexico's provision, N.M. Stat. Ann. § 13-14-25(I) (Supp. 3, 1973), which explicitly bars all other proceedings after an adjudication has begun, is unique. Other states have not been quick to follow New Mexico's lead.

The Supreme Court of California anticipated *Breed v. Jones* by explicitly recognizing the combined effect of *Benton* and *Gault* in *M. v. Superior Court*, 482 P.2d 664 (Cal. 1971). Without dissent that court held that the constitutional guarantee against double jeopardy prohibited multiple threats of judgment in juvenile court proceedings. *Id.* at 668.

The United States Court of Appeals for the Fifth Circuit, in a decision quoted by the Supreme Court in *Breed v. Jones*, also anticipated *Breed*. In *Fain v. Duff*, 488 F.2d 218 (5th Cir. 1973), Fain, arrested for rape in Florida, was indicted in criminal court after a juvenile court had adjudicated him delinquent on the basis of the alleged rape. Before criminal trial, Fain sought and obtained a writ of habeas corpus in federal court, claiming that the indictment placed him twice in jeopardy. The state appealed.

Judge Morgan, speaking for the majority, rejected the notion that there is no jeopardy in a court seeking to rehabilitate:

> Fain's commitment . . . resulted from his having been found delinquent. And his being found delinquent resulted from his having violated a criminal law. . . . Thus a violation of the criminal law may directly result in incarceration. This is a classic example of jeopardy. *Id.* at 225.

Standard 2.1 F. accepts the reasoning of *Breed v. Jones*. The threat of a juvenile court adjudication constitutes jeopardy. The juvenile court judge should not consider waiver of jurisdiction after an adjudicatory hearing has begun.

2.2 Necessary findings.

A. The juvenile court should waive its jurisdiction only upon finding:

1. that probable cause exists to believe that the juvenile has committed the class one or class two juvenile offense alleged in the petition; and

2. that by clear and convincing evidence the juvenile is not a proper person to be handled by the juvenile court.

Commentary

Standard 2.2 A. establishes a two-part test for waiver of juveniles to the criminal court. The juvenile court must find that probable cause exists to believe that the juvenile committed a class one or class two juvenile offense and, by clear and convincing evidence, that the juvenile is not a proper person for juvenile court handling. The required findings are discussed in the commentary following Standards 2.2 B. and 2.2 C.

2.2 B. A finding of probable cause to believe that a juvenile has committed a class one or class two juvenile offense should be based solely on evidence admissible in an adjudicatory hearing of the juvenile court.

Commentary

Standard 2.2 A. requires a probable cause finding as a necessary precondition of waiver. Probable cause is a condition for waiver in eighteen of the thirty-six jurisdictions which have waiver statutes. See, *e.g.*, Me. Rev. Stat. Ann. tit. 15, § 2611(3) (1964), N.C. Gen. Stat. § 7A–280 (1969), and Tex. Family Code § 54.02(f) (1973). The presumption in favor of juvenile court jurisdiction should be overcome only in extreme cases. A juvenile against whom probable cause cannot be found should not be considered an extreme case. A probable cause finding should be a necessary, but not the sole, condition for waiver.

The juvenile court could assume the prosecutor's factual allegations, leaving open only the question of whether a juvenile is a proper person for juvenile court handling. Such a procedure would lead to wasted effort. Inquiry into whether a juvenile is a proper person for juvenile court handling must be careful and thorough to be meaningful. That inquiry is useless if lack of probable cause will

bar any subsequent proceeding, whether criminal or juvenile. Judicial
economy is an important objective. Probable cause is likely to be a
factor in waiver proceedings in all juvenile courts, regardless of the
applicable statutory provisions.

Requiring a probable cause finding at the waiver hearing encourages reliable factual allegations by the prosecutor. A prosecutorial
tactic for overreaching the juvenile in plea bargaining is to threaten
treatment as an adult. That threat can be particularly effective when
the prosecutor can inflate the potential criminal charge without
jeopardizing the case for waiver. Forcing the juvenile to bargain
under such circumstances is unfair.

The juvenile court must find probable cause to believe that the
juvenile's alleged conduct constitutes a class one or class two juvenile
offense. The term "class one juvenile offense" is defined in the *Juvenile Delinquency and Sanctions* volume as those criminal offenses for
which the maximum sentence for adults would be death or imprisonment for life or a term in excess of twenty years. A "class two juvenile offense" would be punishable for adults by imprisonment for
more than five but no more than twenty years. Fourteen of the
states which permit waiver bar surrender of jurisdiction over conduct
amounting only to a misdemeanor. See, *e.g.*, Fla. Stat. Ann. § 39.02
(6)(a) (Supp. 1A, 1973), N.H. Rev. Stat. Ann. § 169:21-a (Supp. 2,
1973), Ohio Rev. Code § 2151.26(A) (Supp. 21, 1973), and Utah
Code Ann. § 55-10-86 (1973).

Juveniles should be waived to the criminal court only when serious
felonies are alleged. Offenses which the legislature has elected to
punish with the severe penalties attached to class one or class two
juvenile offenses should include such serious felonies. Allegations of
lesser criminal acts should be insufficient to overcome the presumption in favor of juvenile court jurisdiction. The class one or class two
juvenile offense requirement limits the prosecutor's ability to inflate
a misdemeanor or minor felony into a major felony to support a
waiver motion. In such a situation, the court could find probable
cause to believe that the juvenile committed the conduct alleged but
that such conduct did not constitute a class one or class two juvenile
offense. The juvenile court could thereby limit prosecutorial manipu-
lation of its jurisdiction.

The probable cause determination must be based on evidence admissible in juvenile court adjudicatory hearings. Evidence which
could not be the basis for an adjudication should not be the basis for
waiver. Concern for judicial economy compels that requirement.
Probable cause determinations based on evidence not otherwise admissible in juvenile court adjudicatory proceedings (or in the criminal

court where evidence standards will be at least as strict) will inevitably result in wasted effort. Standard 2.2 D. permits use of probable cause determinations in waiver proceedings in other juvenile court proceedings. The possibility of multiple use of the waiver probable cause finding necessarily requires that the finding be based on evidence that the juvenile court can otherwise properly consider.

2.2 C. A finding that a juvenile is not a proper person to be handled by the juvenile court must include determinations, by clear and convincing evidence, of:
    1. the seriousness of the alleged class one or class two juvenile offense;
    2. a prior record of adjudicated delinquency involving the infliction or threat of significant bodily injury, if the juvenile is alleged to have committed a class two juvenile offense;
    3. the likely inefficacy of the dispositions available to the juvenile court as demonstrated by previous dispositions of the juvenile; and
    4. the appropriateness of the services and dispositional alternatives available in the criminal justice system for dealing with the juvenile's problems, and whether they are, in fact, available.
Expert opinion should be considered in assessing the likely efficacy of the dispositions available to the juvenile court. A finding that a juvenile is not a proper person to be handled by the juvenile court should be based solely on evidence admissible in a disposition hearing of the juvenile court, and should be in writing, as provided in Standard 2.1 E.

Commentary

The juvenile court should waive jurisdiction only over extraordinary juveniles in extraordinary factual circumstances. Standard 2.2 C. defines those circumstances. Waiver is appropriate only when the juvenile is accused of a serious class one or class two juvenile offense, has demonstrated a propensity for violent acts against other persons and, on the basis of personal background, appears unlikely to benefit from any disposition available to the juvenile court. The court's finding that the juvenile is not a proper person to be handled by the juvenile court should be set forth in a written decision stating the reasons for that conclusion, including the evidence on which it relied, as required in Standard 2.1 E.

Although certain rehabilitative functions are appropriate to the juvenile justice system, existing research suggests a skeptical view of the system's ability to rehabilitate troubled and troublesome juveniles. From the perspective that coercive state intervention in children's lives should be infrequent and limited, the juvenile court has one unarguable advantage; a person subject to the juvenile court is not, unless waived, subject to the harsher penalties of criminal court.

The presumption of Standard 2.2 C., that juveniles should be handled by the juvenile court, accords both with a noninterventionist philosophy and with the conviction that the juvenile court plays a constructive role in the lives of all or some of the juveniles who come within its jurisdiction. The requirements of Standard 2.2 C. must be met before that presumption can be overcome.

Standards 2.2 A. and 2.2 C. speak of juveniles who are not "proper persons to be handled by the juvenile court." A more frequently used concept, premised on a rehabilitative juvenile court rationale, is the juvenile who is not "amenable to treatment." The findings required by Standard 2.2 C. are appropriate regardless of whether or not a rehabilitative view is taken of the juvenile courts.

Twenty-four of the thirty-six jurisdictions that have waiver statutes require a waiver finding that the juvenile is not amenable to treatment. However, nonamenability is not the most widely adopted statutory justification for waiver of juvenile court jurisdiction. Twenty-seven states' statutes establish the "public interest" as a basis for waiver.

Standard 2.2 C. rejects the public interest as a justification for waiver. The presumption in favor of juvenile court jurisdiction requires that the juvenile "deserve" waiver. Waiver must be justified on the basis of the juvenile and his or her actions and personal history. A "public interest" basis for waiver looks to something external to the juvenile. To the extent that the public interest means political considerations, these standards reject such considerations as a proper element in the decision to waive jurisdiction over a specific juvenile. Such factors may be proper considerations for the prosecuting attorney to weigh in deciding whether to seek waiver. They are inappropriate to the waiver decision itself.

Some statutes authorize consideration of general deterrence in waiver proceedings. Montana permits waiver when "the seriousness of the offense and the protection of the community requires treatment of the youth beyond that afforded by juvenile facilities." Mont. Rev. Codes Ann. § 10–2229(d) (Supp. 1 Part 2, 1974). Several states combine considerations of general deterrence with the child's interest. Utah approves waiver when "it would be contrary to the best interests of the child or of the public to retain jurisdiction." Utah Code Ann. § 55-10-86 (1973).

A waiver system premised solely on general deterrence would probably be unconstitutional. The state does not possess authority to use individuals as symbols without regard to individual responsibility. A waiver scheme premised solely on general deterrence would refer some individuals to the criminal court arbitrarily without concern for the facts of specific cases and would probably constitute a denial of due process and equal protection. No state is likely to establish such a scheme, but the arguments against consideration of general deterrence in juvenile court, even as only one element of the waiver decision, are equally applicable. The court's mission is the successful maturation, and in some cases reintegration into the community, of troubled juveniles. Considerations of general deterrence are inappropriate to waiver proceedings.

Some waiver tests are premised on specific deterrence and community security. Some public interest provisions focus on deterrence of the particular individual before the juvenile court. In Connecticut, waiver is possible if "the safety of the community requires that the child continue under restraint for a period extending beyond his majority." Conn. Gen. Stat. Ann. § 17-60a (Supp. 10, 1974). Ohio allows waiver when "[t]he safety of the community *may* require that he be placed under legal restraint . . . for the period extending beyond his majority." Ohio Rev. Code Ann. § 2151.26(A)(3)(b) (Supp. 1973) (emphasis added).

Considerations of specific deterrence and community security are implicit in Standard 2.2 C. The "not a proper person" test is designed to identify juveniles who are genuine threats to community safety as evidenced by the seriousness of the present criminal charge, their past violent acts, and their unsuccessful past experience with the juvenile justice system. Standard 2.2 C. will not authorize waiver over all persons as to whom a persuasive specific deterrence argument could be made. That is a cost that Standard 2.2 C. (and the existence of the juvenile court) evidences willingness to accept.

A judgment that treatment as a juvenile is improper is necessarily subjective. Any subjective decision creates an opportunity for abuse. Juvenile court judges might waive jurisdiction while speaking in terms of nonamenability or not a proper person but thinking of the public interest, general deterrence, or some other inappropriate justification. Limited research on waiver suggests this potential for abuse. Surveys in Wisconsin and Ohio show that a desire to consolidate the trials of juvenile and adult co-offenders often leads to waiver. See

Note, "Waiver of Jurisdiction in Wisconsin Juvenile Courts," 1968 *Wis. L. Rev.* 551, 553 (1968); Note, "Waiver of Jurisdiction in Juvenile Courts," 30 *Ohio St. L. J.* 132, 137 (1969). The United States Children's Bureau's *Survey of Juvenile Courts and Probation Services* (1966) corroborates this finding. Administrative convenience is not an acceptable justification for waiver. That juvenile court judges occasionally accept it demonstrates the opportunities for abuse in waiver decisions.

Subsections 1., 2., and 3. of Standard 2.2 C. contain the specific determinations on which a finding that a juvenile is not a proper person for juvenile court handling must be based. Specific required determinations lessen the likelihood that a juvenile will be waived for public interest, general deterrence, or other inappropriate reasons. Subsection 1. requires that the juvenile be charged with a "serious" class one or class two juvenile offense. In most cases, the probable cause finding required by Standard 2.2 B. will also suffice for 2.2 C. 1. Class one and class two juvenile offenses are defined by the maximum sanctions that may be imposed. Most offenses likely to fall within the categories, such as murder, rape, and armed robbery, will be "serious." Occasionally anomalies will exist. The juvenile court judge should have power to assess the seriousness of the criminal act alleged. If possession of a small quantity of cannabis, or simple theft, is punishable within a jurisdiction by a possible life sentence, the judge should have authority to decide for purposes of waiver that the criminal act alleged is not "serious."

Subsection C.2. requires that the juvenile have been previously adjudicated on charges of threatening or inflicting serious bodily injury if the juvenile is alleged to have committed a class two juvenile offense. The presumption in favor of juvenile court jurisdiction is strong. Only juveniles who pose genuine threats to community safety should be waived and exposed to the greater sanctions of the criminal court. A prior record of violent acts is evidence of that threat. Prior records of property offenses, minor violent offenses, or alleged but unproven serious violent offenses do not evidence that threat. However, it should be noted that an adjudication involving a serious violent offense *by itself* does not warrant waiver. As originally drafted, the standards permitted waiver only if the juvenile was alleged to have committed a class one juvenile offense. When revised to include class two offenses, the requirement of a finding of a prior record was eliminated for class one offenses.

The requirements of subsection 2. probably conform to most present practices. Inconclusive but revealing studies of the Metropolitan Nashville Juvenile Court and Houston's juvenile courts suggest as much. In the Nashville sample, every juvenile remanded to criminal court over a seventeen-month period had appeared in juvenile court at least once before; forty-three of forty-nine had previously been committed. See Note, "Problem of Age and Jurisdiction in the Juvenile Court," 19 *Vand. L. Rev.* 833, 854 (1966). In Houston the juvenile courts considered the waiver of eighteen juveniles over a six-month period. Distributed among those eighteen were twenty-one charges: ten of murder and assault to murder, three of rape, and eight of robbery by firearms. Hays and Solway, "The Role of Psychological Evaluation in Certification of Juveniles for Trial as Adults," 9 *Houston L. Rev.* 709, 710 (1972).

Subsection C. 3. requires the juvenile court judge to consider every available dispositional alternative and the likelihood that the juvenile will not benefit from each. This analysis should include detailed consideration of the juvenile's previous exposure to juvenile justice programs.

In *Haziel v. United States*, 404 F.2d 1275 (D.C. Cir. 1968), a United States Court of Appeals considered the validity of an order, supported by a bare finding of nonamenability, that waived juvenile court jurisdiction. The case was decided on the juvenile court judge's failure to obtain an adequate release by the juvenile of his right to a waiver hearing. The court of appeals nevertheless devoted considerable attention to the sufficiency of the waiver findings. Chief Judge Bazelon wrote:

> The Juvenile Court did not indicate what strategy might offer hope to rehabilitate the appellant, nor what facilities would be necessary to pursue such a strategy nor what efforts had been made to explore the availability of such facilities. The unelaborated conclusion that "facilities currently available to the Juvenile Court" offered no promise of rehabilitation thus telescoped together the several distinct stages of this critical inquiry. *Id.* at 1280.

Faced with a suspicious waiver order, the juvenile court was warned not to "abandon its statutory duty to help the young offender." *Id.* at 1282. The court of appeals required that an examination of all dispositional alternatives precede any finding of nonamenability. "[I]t is only after all rehabilitative possibilities have been canvassed that a decision to waive jurisdiction to the District Court is ever proper." *Id.*

The *Haziel* requirements ensure a thorough, particularized study of the juvenile's situation and discourage cursory consideration of dispositional alternatives. Subsection C. 3. seeks to achieve the same ends. Recurrent examination of dispositional alternatives may focus attention on the juvenile court's facilities and contribute to their improvement. "Perhaps it is only by searching for what we need but do not have that future improvements in knowledge and resources can be hoped for." *Id.* at 1280.

Standard 2.2 C. encourages consideration of expert opinion in assessing the likely efficacy of the dispositions available to the juvenile court.

The court may find that a juvenile is not a proper person for juvenile court handling only on the basis of clear and convincing evidence. This provision is a compromise between the widely used standard of proof of the justification for waiver by a preponderance of the evidence and the beyond-a-reasonable-doubt standard required in juvenile adjudications.

Use of the standard constitutionally required in juvenile court adjudicatory hearings would unduly restrict the juvenile court's power to waive jurisdiction. Determinations that a juvenile is not a "proper person" are exercises in judgment of the sort never entirely free from reasonable doubt. A lesser standard, which nonetheless requires a thorough demonstration of the need for waiver—which a mere preponderance test does not—is appropriate. For this reason, the standard of proof by clear and convincing evidence has been chosen.

The findings required by Standard 2.2 C. must be based on evidence admissible in a juvenile court dispositional hearing. Evidence that cannot properly be considered by the juvenile court at a dispositional hearing following an adjudication is no more credible or worthy of consideration in the context of waiver.

A finding that a juvenile is not a proper person for juvenile court handling must include all four determinations required by Standard 2.2 C. Only extraordinary juveniles in extraordinary circumstances should be waived. If any of the required determinations cannot be made on the basis of clear and convincing evidence, the juvenile should not be waived. Standard 2.2 C. permits but does not require waiver. The juvenile need not be waived even if the juvenile court judge decides that all four determinations have been demonstrated by clear and convincing evidence.

2.2 D. A finding of probable cause to believe that a juvenile has committed a class one or class two juvenile offense may be substituted for a probable cause determination relating to that offense (or a lesser included offense) required in any subsequent juvenile court proceeding. Such a finding should not be substituted for any finding of probable cause required in any subsequent criminal proceeding.

Commentary

Standard 2.2 D. bars substitution of the waiver hearing's finding of probable cause for any similar finding required in any subsequent criminal proceeding. The bar does not apply to subsequent juvenile court proceedings.

Many jurisdictions have limited provisions for discovery in criminal proceedings. In the words of Judge Weinstein, a preliminary hearing constitutes "the most valuable discovery technique available" to the criminal defendant. *United States ex rel. Wheeler v. Flood*, 269 F. Supp. 194, 198 (E.D.N.Y. 1967). Depriving the person waived from juvenile court jurisdiction of this opportunity to learn the nature of the evidence gathered is unfair and possibly unconstitutional. The juvenile will often have stipulated the existence of probable cause at the waiver hearing and focused on the issue of being a proper person for juvenile court handling.

The juvenile court situation is different. Principles of economy favor consolidation of judicial function. The court, the juvenile, the prosecuting attorney, and the issues are the same in probable cause determinations in the context of waiver and in other juvenile court contexts. Neither the juvenile court nor the juvenile should be required to go through the same motions a second time. *Breed v. Jones*, 421 U.S. 519 (1975), does not require otherwise.

2.3 The hearing.
A. The juvenile should be represented by counsel at the waiver hearing. The clerk of the juvenile court should give written notice to the juvenile, multilingual if appropriate, of this requirement at least [five] court days before commencement of the waiver hearing.

Commentary

Standard 2.3 A. requires that the juvenile be represented by counsel. Written notice of the requirement, multilingual if appropriate, must be given to the juvenile at least [five] court days before the waiver hearing begins.

Kent v. United States, 383 U.S. 541 (1966), acknowledges the constitutional significance of the right to counsel in waiver proceedings: "The right to representation by counsel is not a formality. It is not a grudging gesture to a ritualistic requirement. It is of the essence of justice." *Id.* at 561. This right has been widely acknowledged.

See, *e.g.*, Alaska R. Juv. P. 3(c) and 15(a); *Steinhauser v. State*, 206 S.2d 25 (Fla. 1967); and N.D. Cent. Code § 27-20-26 (1974).

This standard rejects, for the juvenile court, the Supreme Court's decision in *Faretta v. California*, 422 U.S. 806 (1975). *Faretta* affirms the constitutional right of an adult criminal defendant to represent him- or herself without benefit of counsel.

Some, perhaps all, juveniles may be legally incapable of a knowing and intelligent waiver of the right to counsel. The thirteen-year-old is unlikely to have sufficient maturity and perspective. The seventeen-year-old may. Any method of determining which juveniles are capable of an intelligent and knowing waiver of the right to counsel will inevitably err on occasion. Rather than accept the inevitable error, Standard 2.3 A. imposes counsel on the hypothetical juvenile who rejects the right to counsel.

A fundamental premise of this volume is that juveniles are different from adults in material respects. Being a juvenile should seldom justify reduced procedural protections. That state does justify the imposition of a protection which should in most cases benefit the juvenile.

2.3 B. **The juvenile court should appoint counsel to represent any juvenile unable to afford representation by counsel at the waiver hearing. The clerk of the juvenile court should give written notice to the juvenile, multilingual if appropriate, of this right at least [five] court days before commencement of the waiver hearing.**

Commentary

Standard 2.3 B. requires appointment of counsel to represent juveniles unable to afford representation at the waiver hearing.

Since *In re Gault*, 387 U.S. 1 (1967), juveniles unarguably have a constitutional right to counsel, including appointed counsel when necessary, in any juvenile court adjudicatory hearing.

A similar constitutional right to counsel must exist for waiver hearings. An adverse decision results in denial of juvenile court handling and its limited sanctions, and in prosecution, conviction, and punishment as an adult. The need for procedural protection in waiver proceedings was recognized before *Kent v. United States*, 383 U.S. 541 (1966), and the *Gault* opinions were issued. In *Black v. United States*, the United States Court of Appeals for the District of Columbia observed that the need for the assistance of counsel, while substantial in delinquency hearings, "is even greater in the adjudication of waiver since it contemplates the imposition of criminal sanctions." 355 F.2d 104, 106 (D.C. Cir. 1965). Also see *Kemplen v. Maryland*, 428 F.2d 169, 173–75 (4th Cir. 1970).

The propriety of notification of the right to counsel is indisputable. *Gault* requires such notice in juvenile adjudications, 387 U.S. at 41, and *Kemplen* explicitly extended the requirements to waiver hearings. 428 F.2d at 175.

2.3 C. The juvenile court should pay the reasonable fees and expenses of an expert witness for the juvenile if the juvenile desires, but is unable to afford, the services of such an expert witness at the waiver hearing, unless the presiding officer determines that the expert witness is not necessary.

Commentary

Standard 2.3 C. requires the juvenile court to pay the reasonable costs and expenses of an expert witness for the juvenile in cases of indigency, unless the court exercises its discretion to rule that no need appears for such testimony.

Standard 2.2 C. 3. requires the waiver judge to consider the likely efficacy of available juvenile court dispositions in deciding whether a juvenile is a proper person for juvenile court handling. Standard 2.2 C. also requires the juvenile court judge to consider expert opinion in considering the 2.2 C. 3. finding. The juvenile should receive benefit of the testimony of experts chosen by the defense, even when the juvenile cannot afford the expert's fees and expenses.

Wealth should not determine the quality of a juvenile's opposition to waiver. Justice Black eloquently affirmed the necessity of "providing equal justice for poor and rich . . . alike" in the majority opinion in *Griffin v. Illinois*, 351 U.S. 12 (1956). *Griffin* involved indigent criminal defendants who were denied free transcripts for use in appellate proceedings:

> Surely no one could contend that either a State or the Federal Government could constitutionally provide that defendants unable to pay court costs in advance should be denied the right to plead not guilty or to defend themselves in court. Such a law would make the constitutional promise of a fair trial a worthless thing. Notice, the right to be heard, and the right to counsel would under such circumstances be meaningless promises to the poor. In criminal trials a State can no more discriminate on account of poverty than on account of religion, race or color. *Id.* at 16–17.

In *Jacobs v. United States*, 320 F.2d 571 (4th Cir. 1965), citing *Griffin*, the fourth circuit extended this guarantee to include court appointment of a psychiatrist to testify on defendant's competency to stand trial. In 1969 the seventh circuit extended *Griffin* to juvenile adjudications. *Reed v. Duter*, 416 F.2d 744 (7th Cir. 1969). Given *Jacobs* and *Reed*, the requirement that the state pay the costs of an expert witness in waiver proceedings is consistent with current constitutional precepts.

2.3 D. The juvenile should have access to all evidence available to the juvenile court which could be used either to support or contest the waiver motion.

Commentary

Standard 2.3 D. grants the juvenile access to all evidence available to the juvenile court that could be used to support or contest the waiver motion.

Justice Fortas in *Kent v. United States*, 383 U.S. 541 (1966), asserted a District of Columbia juvenile's right to access through his attorney to all information in the hands of the juvenile court:

> With respect to access by the child's counsel to the social records of the child, we deem it obvious that since these are to be considered by the juvenile court in making its decision to waive, they must be made available to the child's counsel. 383 U.S. at 562.

An eminent scholar soon responded, criticizing this holding as a "shortcoming." Paulsen, "*Kent v. United States:* The Constitutional Context of Juvenile Cases," 1966 *Sup. Ct. Rev.* 167, 179-81. Paulsen argued that the Supreme Court underestimated the importance of juvenile court confidentiality, fearing that full disclosure of social records would "touch off an uproar among social workers." He noted:

> There is a footnote referring to the fact that Kent's lawyer had, in fact, seen the confidential material at a stage in the proceedings after the waiver decision. In that footnote, Mr. Justice Fortas quipped: "Perhaps the point of it is that it again illustrates the maxim that while nondisclosure may contribute to the comfort of the staff, disclosure does not cause the heavens to fall." To which many experienced probation officers would respond: "Not right away perhaps." *Id.* at 179-80.

Paulsen feared that the disclosure requirement would dry up one of the juvenile court's principal sources of information:

> To get information, especially of an intimate sort, the social investigator must be able to give firm assurances of confidentiality; if people generally learn that supplying information will bring them to court or plunge them into a neighborhood feud, they will no longer share their knowledge and impressions; information destructive of the youngster's chances at rehabilitation may' leak back to him. *Id.* at 180.

The decade since *Kent* has seen no revolt by juvenile court personnel in the District of Columbia or nationwide. Social workers have adjusted well to *Kent's* imposition on the confidentiality of their reports. Paulsen underestimated the ability of juvenile court personnel to adjust to full disclosure in the waiver setting. That demonstrated ability is a persuasive argument for *Kent's* disclosure requirements.

2.3 E. The prosecuting attorney should bear the burden of proving that probable cause exists to believe that the juvenile has committed a class one or class two juvenile offense and that the juvenile is not a proper person to be handled by the juvenile court.

F. The juvenile may contest the waiver motion by challenging, or producing evidence tending to challenge, the evidence of the prosecuting attorney.

G. The juvenile may examine any person who prepared any report concerning the juvenile which is presented at the waiver hearing.

H. All evidence presented at the waiver hearing should be under oath and subject to cross-examination.

Commentary

Standard 2.3 E. through H. establishes requirements for the conduct of the waiver hearing. The waiver hearing will determine whether a juvenile is denied juvenile court handling or is exposed to the practices and punishments of the criminal court. A decision of that magnitude should be considered on the basis of a fully adversary hearing in which the state must establish the propriety of the result that it urges. The prosecutor should bear the burden of proof and the risk of nonpersuasion. The juvenile should be able to contest prosecution evidence; cross-examine prosecution witnesses, including persons who prepare reports which the prosecution introduces in support of waiver; and present original evidence in opposition to waiver. On the right to compulsory process, see *Dispositional Procedures* Standard 6.2, *Juvenile Records and Information Systems* Standard 5.7 B., and *Pretrial Court Proceedings* Standard 1.5 F.

2.3 I. The juvenile may remain silent at the waiver hearing. No admission by the juvenile during the waiver hearing should be admissible to establish guilt or to impeach testimony in any subsequent proceeding, except a perjury proceeding.

Commentary

Standard 2.3 I. establishes a right to silence in waiver hearings. The juvenile's right to silence at the waiver hearing should be axiomatic. The Supreme Court recognized this right in juvenile adjudications in *In re Gault*, 387 U.S. 1 (1967), and in criminal prosecutions in *Malloy v. Hogan*, 378 U.S. 1 (1964). The protection against self-incrimination available in the juvenile and criminal courts should apply to the hearing which serves as the bridge between them.

Standard 2.3 I. also gives the juvenile power to bar the introduction in any subsequent criminal trial or other proceeding, except for perjury, of admissions made during the waiver hearing.

Twenty states offer similar evidentiary protection to juveniles opposing waiver. These statutes fall into three general categories. Some, like Va. Code Ann. § 16.1-176(b) (Supp. 4, 1974) and Wyo. Stat. Ann. § 14-115.38 (Supp. 5, 1973), appear as part of the statute authorizing waiver and apply solely to that process. Others, like Ala. Code tit. 13, § 377 (1959) and Ore. Rev. Stat. § 419.567(3) (1974), apply to all juvenile court proceedings, including waiver hearings. Still others seem to pertain to waiver, but ambiguous drafting (resulting, perhaps, from a preoccupation with admissions at other juvenile court hearings) clouds the issue. See, *e.g.*, Mass. Ann. Laws ch. 119, § 60 (Supp. 18, 1974) and Mich. Comp. Laws Ann. § 712A.23 (1969). A statute specifically applicable to admission at the waiver hearing is preferable.

Such statutes encourage candor at the waiver hearing. A better-informed waiver decision should result. The juvenile need not fear that an admission of misconduct—contrition evidencing that the juvenile is a proper person for juvenile court handling—will lead to a criminal conviction if the juvenile court elects to waive jurisdiction.

Justice Harlan offered similar reasoning in an analogous situation in *Simmons v. United States*, 390 U.S. 377 (1968). One co-defendant admitted ownership of a suitcase in order to establish standing to suppress evidence found in the suitcase; at trial this admission was used against him. The defendant claimed that such use had a chilling effect on his right to challenge the introduction of evidence unconstitutionally seized.

The Supreme Court agreed:

> [T]here will be a deterrent effect in those . . . cases in which it cannot be estimated with confidence whether the motion will succeed. Since search-and-seizure claims depend heavily upon their individual facts, and since the law of search and seizure is in a state of flux, the incidence of such marginal cases cannot be said to be negligible. *Id.* at 393.

The *Simmons* opinion observes that, in marginal suppression cases "a defendant with a substantial claim for the exclusion of evidence may conclude that the admission of the evidence, together with the Government's proof linking it to him, is preferable to risking the admission of his own testimony connecting himself with the seized evidence." *Id.* at 393. Most waiver cases are marginal. The juvenile with an argument against waiver based in part on inferences from an admission of misconduct might accept a criminal trial after token opposition to waiver rather than risk use of such an admission at a criminal trial. Standard 2.3 E. avoids this dilemma for the juvenile. Use of admissions during the waiver process in subsequent criminal proceedings is prohibited.

The 2.3 I. restriction does not apply to subsequent juvenile proceedings. Similarly, Standard 2.2 D. permits subsequent use in the juvenile court of the waiver hearing's probable cause determination.

The primary reason for permitting later juvenile court use of admissions at the waiver hearing is judicial economy. Otherwise, a juvenile could admit (or the court could find probable cause to believe) occurrence of a class one juvenile offense but assert innocence at a juvenile court probable cause or adjudicatory hearing. The court, the juvenile, the prosecutor, and defense counsel would have to consider probable cause de novo or try a question that all believe has previously been resolved.

Standard 2.3 I.'s evidentiary bar is broad. Admissions made during the waiver hearing may not be used either to establish guilt or to impeach testimony.

Standard 2.3 I. rejects the distinction in *Harris v. New York*, 401 U.S. 222 (1971), between inadmissible use of the defendant's statements to establish guilt (because obtained without proper *Miranda* warnings) and admissible use to attack the credibility of the defendant's testimony in his or her own behalf.

2.3 J. The juvenile may disqualify the presiding officer at the waiver hearing from presiding at any subsequent criminal trial or juvenile court adjudicatory hearing relating to any transaction or episode alleged in the petition initiating juvenile court proceedings.

Commentary

Standard 2.3 J. permits the juvenile to disqualify the judge who presided at the waiver hearing from presiding at a subsequent juvenile court adjudication or criminal trial.

The waiver judge hears evidence that would be inadmissible in an adjudicatory hearing or a trial. The likelihood that the juvenile will perceive impropriety is great. Standard 2.3 J. permits any juvenile who senses such a disadvantage to demand a different judge at the adjudicatory proceeding.

Similar provisions appear at § 31 (i) of the "Legislative Guide for Drafting Family and Juvenile Court Acts" prepared by the United States Children's Bureau and at § 34(E) of the Uniform Juvenile Court Act. The notes of the National Conference of Commissioners on Uniform Laws appended to subsection (E) offer this rationale:

> On a hearing to transfer, the judge of necessity must hear and consider matters relating adversely to the child which would be inadmissible in a hearing on the merits of the petition. Hence, the need for avoiding their prejudicial effect by requiring over objection that another judge hear the charges made in the petition or in the criminal court if the case is transferred.

The commissioners emphasize the danger of actual prejudice to the juvenile. This danger is less persuasive an argument for disqualification than is the certainty of apparent prejudice. No matter how fair the waiver judge may be in subsequent proceedings, an impression of unfairness will exist.

2.4 Appeal.

A. The juvenile or the prosecuting attorney may file an appeal of the waiver decision with the court authorized to hear appeals from final judgments of the juvenile court within [seven] court days of the decision of the juvenile court.

Commentary

The right to appeal provided by Standard 2.4 A. must be exercised within [seven] court days after the waiver decision. The alternative—review only after entry of a final order in either criminal or juvenile court—appears to be the majority rule. Few statutes address the issue. State courts have disagreed sharply. *Appeals and Collateral Review* Standard 2.2 C. 2. e. expressly authorizes appeal of the waiver decision.

The leading exponent of the majority rule is *People v. Jiles*, 251 N.E.2d 529 (Ill. 1969). The Supreme Court of Illinois refused a petition for immediate review of waiver, citing standard arguments against interlocutory appeals:

> To permit interlocutory review of such an order would obviously delay the prosecution of any proceeding in either the juvenile or the criminal division, with the result that the prospect of a just disposition would be jeopardized. In either proceeding the primary issue is the ascertainment of the innocence or guilt of the person charged. To permit interlocutory review would subordinate that primary issue and defer its consideration. . . . *Id*. at 531.

Similar decisions include *Brekke v. People*, 233 Cal. App. 2d 196, 43 Cal. Rptr. 553 (1965), and *In re T.J.H.*, 479 S.W.2d 433 (Mo. 1972).

The supreme courts of Oregon, Tennessee, and Hawaii have approved interlocutory appeal from waiver decisions. *State v. Little*, 407 P.2d 627 (Ore. 1965); *In re Houston*, 428 S.W.2d 303 (Tenn. 1968); and *In re Doe I*, 444 P.2d 459 (Hawaii 1968).

The principal advantage of immediate appeal is avoidance of the reconstructed waiver hearing, the proceeding necessary when an appellate court finds a defect in the original waiver hearing after the person waived is, because of the time consumed by the criminal trial, beyond the age jurisdiction of the juvenile court. The appellate court which upholds a waiver appeal must either free the improperly waived individual—because neither juvenile nor criminal court has jurisdiction—or reconstruct the waiver process to determine if a hearing free from error would have resulted in waiver. The reconstructed hearing must attempt to imagine the juvenile as he or she was at the time of the original hearing.

The experience of Morris Kent illustrates the problems that arise when interlocutory appeal from waiver decisions is not possible. Kent was apprehended at age sixteen on September 5, 1961. Waived to criminal court seven days later, he sought immediate appellate review. He appealed to the municipal court of appeals, then the highest local court in the District of Columbia. He sought a writ of habeas corpus in United States District Court. The district court dismissed the application for the writ on September 19, 1961, and rejected the appeal on April 13, 1962. *In re Kent*, 179 A.2d 727 (1962). On January 22, 1963, the court of appeals for the District of Columbia held that a motion to dismiss Kent's criminal indictment was the proper vehicle for challenging the waiver decision and that denial of such a motion was reviewable only after conviction. *Kent v. Reid*, 316 F.2d 331 (D.C. Cir. 1963). Morris Kent was still within the age jurisdiction of the juvenile court.

The district court denied Kent's motion to dismiss the indictment on February 8, 1963. Kent was convicted of robbery. He appealed to the court of appeals, which finally heard his attack on the juvenile court's waiver of jurisdiction on December 17, 1963—twenty-seven months after the fact.

That court affirmed Kent's conviction in 1964 and denied rehearing en banc in early 1965. *Kent v. United States*, 343 F.2d 247 (D.C. Cir. 1965). The Supreme Court granted certiorari in 1965. The landmark decision was issued on March 21, 1966. Justice Fortas recognized the difficulty of providing appropriate relief to Kent, by then over twenty-one:

> In view of the unavailability of a redetermination of the waiver question by the Juvenile Court, it is urged by petitioner that the conviction should be vacated and the indictment dismissed. In the circumstances of this case . . . , we do not consider it appropriate to grant this drastic relief. Accordingly, we vacate the order of the Court of Appeals and the judgment of the District Court and remand the case to the District Court for a hearing *de novo* on waiver, consistent with this opinion. 383 U.S. 541, 564–65 (1966).

The Supreme Court thereby sanctioned the reconstructed waiver hearing.

The case reports do not indicate the precise date on which the district court attempted to transform itself into a juvenile court sitting in September 1961. The reconstructed hearing probably occurred in the latter half of 1966. Removed almost five years from his previous circumstances, Kent agreed that juvenile treatment would have been inappropriate in 1961 but argued that civil commitment, not waiver into criminal court, would have been the best disposition.

The district court in 1967 rejected this contention, finding waiver reasonable in the circumstances. The court of appeals reversed the lower court on July 30, 1968. *Kent v. United States*, 401 F.2d 408

(D.C. Cir. 1968). Kent thus first obtained substantive appellate review of a procedurally adequate waiver decision more than eighty-two months after the juvenile court had waived its jurisdiction.

The delay caused by deferring appeal of waiver aggravates the impossibility at any reconstructed hearing of ignoring present conditions. Reconstructed waiver hearings ask judges to do what may be impossible and what certainly is unwise.

Congress alleviated the need for such hearings by establishing for the District of Columbia a right of immediate appeal of waiver decisions. Had a provision analogous to D.C. Code Ann. § 16-2327 (1973) been in force at the time, the court in *Kent v. Reid* could have ruled on the sufficiency of Kent's waiver. Had the appeals court found a defect, the juvenile court could have reasserted jurisdiction and redetermined waiver. There would have been no reconstructed waiver hearing. Standard 2.4 A. attempts to avoid the *Kent* problem and assure a similar result in all jurisdictions.

Standard 2.4 A. also provides that the court that normally reviews final judgments of the juvenile court should hear appeals regarding waiver of juvenile court jurisdiction. A few states involve the criminal courts in the appellate process, thereby tempting those judges covetous of juvenile court jurisdiction. Such temptation should be avoided.

Waiver of juvenile court jurisdiction in Alaska is first reviewable in the criminal court that will try the juvenile's case. Alaska R. Juv. P. 3(h). In Virginia the prosecutor can appeal a decision *not* to waive to the court that would have tried the case if the juvenile judge had waived jurisdiction. Va. Code Ann. § 16.1-176(e) (Supp. 4, 1974). Either of these provisions requires the criminal court to determine whether its treatment of the juvenile will be preferable to that of the juvenile court. The natural tendency of the criminal court judge is to suppose that criminal court can do the better job.

A more evenhanded view of the jurisdictional claims of criminal and juvenile courts should apply if the court that hears other juvenile court appeals reviews the waiver decision. Such courts of appeal usually review criminal convictions as well as juvenile adjudications. Their deliberations should be relatively unbiased. As appellate courts they are experienced in statutory interpretation and constitutional adjudication.

2.4 B. The appellate court should render its decision expeditiously, according the findings of the juvenile court the same weight given the findings of the highest court of general trial jurisdiction.

Commentary

Standard 2.4 B. requires the appellate court to apply the standard of review customarily applied to the decisions of other courts of original jurisdiction. This provision assures that waiver appeals will be treated no differently from other cases on the appellate court's docket. The probable cause and impropriety determinations of the juvenile court are neither particularly vulnerable nor particularly invulnerable to appellate review.

2.4 C. No criminal court should have jurisdiction in any proceeding relating to any transaction or episode alleged in the juvenile court petition as to which a waiver motion was made, against any person over whom the juvenile court has waived jurisdiction, until the time for filing an appeal from that determination has passed or, if such an appeal has been filed, until the final decision of the appellate court has been issued.

Commentary

Standard 2.4 C. seeks to protect the juvenile from multiple threats of judgment. Appeal of the waiver decision suspends further criminal or juvenile proceedings. Thus there can be no possibility that the appellate court might overturn waiver of juvenile court jurisdiction after criminal jeopardy has attached. D.C. Code Ann. § 16-2327 (1973) has a similar provision.

Bibliography

ARTICLES, NOTES, AND COMMENT

M. Alers, "Transfer of Jurisdiction from Juvenile to Criminal Court," 19 *Crime & Delinq.* 519 (1973).

M. Altman, "Effect of the Miranda Case on Confessions in the Juvenile Court," 5 *Am. Crim. L.Q.* 79 (1967).

L. Arthur, "Uniform Juvenile Court Act," 19 *Juv. Ct. Judges J.* 153 (1969).

K. Atkinson, "Constitutional Rights of Juveniles: Gault and its Application," 9 *Wm. & Mary L. Rev.* 492 (1967).

H. Bellfatto, "Constitution in the Juvenile Court," 13 *N.Y.L.F.* 1 (1967).

H. Berenson, "Lawyer in the Juvenile Court," 38 *J.B.A. Kan.* 15 (1969).

R. Blank, "Constitutional Law: The Jury and the Juvenile Court," 24 *U. Fla. L. Rev.* 385 (1972).

A. Bottoms, McClean, and Patchett, "Children, Young Persons and the Courts: A Survey of the New Law," 1970 *Crim. L. Rev.* 368.

C. Buss, "Waiver of Jurisdiction in Wisconsin Juvenile Courts," 1968 *Wis. L. Rev.* 551.

C. Cadena, "Due Process and the Juvenile Offender," 1 *St. Mary's L.J.* 23 (1969).

M. Carnach and S. Haines, "Juvenile's Right to Bail in Oregon," *Ore. L. Rev.* 194 (1968).

R. Carpenter, "Due Process Dilemma—Juries for Juveniles," 45 *N.D.L. Rev.* 251 (1969).

J. Carr, "Juries for Juveniles: Solving the Dilemma," 2 *Loyola U.L.J.* 1 (1971).

W. Carr, "Juvenile Court v. Due Process: A Comparison," 8 *Ga. St. B.J.* 9 (1971).

L. Carver and White, "Constitutional Safeguards for the Juvenile Offender," 14 *Crime & Delinq.* 63 (1968).

C. Cashman, "Confidentiality of Juvenile Court Proceedings: A Review," 24 *Juv. Justice* 30 (1973).

C. Cayton, "Emerging Patterns in the Administration of Juvenile Justice," 49 *J. Urban L.* 377 (1971).

S. Coxe, "Lawyers in Juvenile Court," 13 *Crime & Delinq.* 488 (1967).

J. Dabrow and Migliore, "Juvenile Rights Under the Fourth Amendment," 11 *J. Family L.* 753 (1972).

G. Davidson, *"In re Gault:* The Juvenile's Gideon," 56 *Ill. B.J.* 488 (1968).

S. Davis, "The Jurisdictional Dilemma of the Juvenile Court," 51 *N.C.L. Rev.* 195 (1972).

S. Davis, "Justice for the Juvenile: The Decision to Arrest and Due Process," 1971 *Duke L.J.* 913 (1971).

M. Dobzon, "Juvenile Court and Parental Rights," 4 *Family L.Q.* 393 (1970).

W. Douglas, "Juvenile Courts and Due Process of Law," 19 *Juv. Ct. Judges J.* 9 (1968).

J. Duffy, *"In re Gault* and the Privilege Against Self-Incrimination in Juvenile Court," 51 *Marq. L. Rev.* 68 (1967).

C. Fairlie, "Appellate Review of Juvenile Court Dispositions: Gault's Forgotten Footnote," 5 *Conn. L. Rev.* 117 (1972).

R. Fazzone, "Juvenile Court Procedures Beyond Gault," 32 *Albany L. Rev.* 126 (1967).

J. Feldman, "Prosecutor's Special Tasks in Juvenile Delinquency Proceedings in Illinois," 59 *Ill. B.J.* 146 (1970).

S. Fox, "Prosecutors in the Juvenile Court: A Statutory Proposal," 8 *Harv. J. Legis.* 33 (1970).

M. Frey, "Criminal Responsibility of the Juvenile Murderer," 1970 *Wash. U.L.Q.* 113.

M. Frey, "Effect of the Gault Decision on the Iowa Juvenile Justice System," 17 *Drake L. Rev.* 53 (1967).

M. Frey, "Evolution of Juvenile Court Jurisdiction and Procedure in Texas," 1 *Tex. Tech. L. Rev.* 209 (1970).

J. Ganzfried, "Double Jeopardy and the Waiver of Jurisdiction in California's Juvenile Courts," 24 *Stan. L. Rev.* 874 (1972).

R. Gardner, "Gault and California," 19 *Hastings L.J.* 527 (1968).

M.C. Garner, "Due Process and Waiver of Juvenile Court Jurisdiction," 30 *Wash. & Lee L. Rev.* 591 (1973).

B. George, "Juvenile Delinquency Proceedings: The Due Process Model," 40 *U. Colo. L. Rev.* 315 (1968).

W. Gersh, "Double Jeopardy and the Juvenile," 11 *J. Family L.* 603 (1972).

J. Glen, "Developments in Juvenile and Family Court Law," 16 *Crime & Delinq.* 198 (1970).

J. Glen, "Developments in Juvenile and Family Court Law," 17 *Crime & Delinq.* 224 (1971).

J. Glen, "Juvenile Court Reform: Procedural Process and Substantive Stasis," 1970 *Wis. L. Rev.* 431 (1970).

A. Gough, "Consent Decrees and Informal Service in the Juvenile Court: Excursions Toward Balance," 19 *U. Kan. L. Rev.* 733 (1971).

B. Green, "Disposition of Juvenile Offenders," 13 *Crim. L.Q.* 348 (1971).

J. Greenspun, "Role of the Attorney in Juvenile Court," 18 *Clev. St. L. Rev.* 599 (1969).

R. Gullick, "Right to Jury Trial: Indiana's Misapplication of Due Process Standards in Delinquency Hearings," 45 *Ind. L.J.* 578 (1970).

R. Habinger, "Prosecution of Children in Missouri Poses Constitutional Problems," 30 *Mo. B.J.* 11 (1974).

A. Hawes, "Gault and the District of Columbia," 17 *Am. U.L. Rev.* 153 (1968).

H. Hayes and K. Solway, "The Role of Psychological Evaluation in Certification of Juveniles for Trial as Adults," 9 *Houston L. Rev.* 709 (1972).

D. Herbert, "Adversary Juvenile Delinquency Proceedings: Impeachment of Juvenile Defendants by the Use of Previous Adjudications of Delinquency," 8 *Akron L. Rev.* 443 (1975).

P. Hosey, "Waiver in Juvenile Proceedings," 23 *Baylor L. Rev.* 467 (1971).

J. Isaacs, "Lawyer in the Juvenile Court," 40 *Crim. L.Q.* 222 (1968).

J. Ishamael, "Juvenile Right to Counsel at Probation Revocation Hearing," 11 *J. Family L.* 745 (1972).

J. Johnson, "Juvenile Court in Transition," 44 *Fla. B.J.* 514 (1970).

B. Joyner and J. Maxey, "Juvenile Offenses: A Study of Adjudication and Disposition in Mississippi," 42 *Miss. L.J.* 60 (1971).

B. Kaliel, "Civil Rights in Juvenile Courts," 12 *Alberta L. Rev.* 341 (1974).

R. Kay and D. Segal, "Role of the Attorney in Juvenile Court Proceedings: A Non-Polar Approach," 61 *Geo. L.J.* 1401 (1973).

H. Keith, "Waiver of Jurisdiction in Juvenile Courts," 30 *Ohio St. L.J.* 132 (1969).

R. Kerl, "Due Process Requirements and Parole Revocation for the Youthful Offender," 10 *Idaho L. Rev.* 275 (1974).

O. Ketcham, "Guidelines from Gault: Revolutionary Requirements and Reappraisal," 53 *Va. L. Rev.* 1700 (1967).

O. Ketcham, "*McKeiver v. Pennsylvania:* The Last Word on Juvenile Court Adjudications?" 57 *Cornell L. Rev.* 561 (1972).

O. Ketcham, "The Unfulfilled Promise of the Juvenile Court," 7 *Crime & Delinq.* 97 (1961).

K. Kolson, "Rural Compliance with Gault: Kentucky, A Case Study," 10 *J. Family L.* 300 (1971).

M. Kravitz, "Due Process in Ohio for the Delinquent and Unruly Child," 2 *Capital U.L. Rev.* 53 (1973).

M. Lawton, "Juvenile Proceedings—The New Look," 20 *Am. U.L. Rev.* 342 (1971).

N. Lefstein, "*In re Gault:* Juvenile Courts and Lawyers," 53 *A.B.A.J.* 811 (1967).

H. Lenon, "On Re-examining Gault—Again and Again," 4 *Family L.Q.* 387 (1970).

N. Levin, "Role of the Lawyer in Juvenile Proceedings," 39 *Pa. B.A.Q.* 427 (1968).

W. MacFaden, "Changing Concepts of Juvenile Justice," 17 *Crime and Delinq.* 131 (1971).

G. Marcovsky, "Double Jeopardy and Due Process in the Juvenile Courts," 29 *U. Pitt. L. Rev.* 756 (1968).

C. McCarter, "Constitutional Rights of Juveniles in Criminal Cases—Gault and Beyond in North Carolina," 7 *Wake Forest L. Rev.* 440 (1971).

T. McMillan and D. McMurtry, "Role of the Defense Lawyer in the Juvenile Court—Advocate or Social Worker?" 14 *St. Louis U.L.J.* 561 (1970).

R. Mennel, "Origins of the Juvenile Court: Changing Perspectives on the Legal Rights of Juvenile Delinquents," 18 *Crime & Delinq.* 68 (1972).

C. Merz, "Representing the Juvenile Defendant in Waiver Proceedings," 12 *St. Louis U.L.J.* 424 (1968).

M. Midonick and Sonderlich, "Children Before the Bench," 10 *Trial* 38 (1974).

J. Miller, "Dilemma of the Post-Gault Juvenile Court," 3 *Family L.Q.* 229 (1969).

M. Milton, "Post-Gault: A New Prospectus for the Juvenile Court," 16 *N.Y.L.F.* 57 (1970).

J. Mogilner, "Admissibility of Evidence in Juvenile Court—A Double Standard or No Standard," 46 *Cal. St. B.J.* 310 (1971).

S. Mora, "Juvenile Detention: A Constitutional Problem Affecting Local Government," 1 *Urban Lawyer* 189 (1969).

H. Mountford and H. Berenson, "Waiver of Jurisdiction: The Last Resort of the Juvenile Court," 18 *U. Kan. L. Rev.* 55 (1969).

J. Mudd, "Constitution and Juvenile Delinquents," 32 *Mont. L. Rev.* 307 (1971).

P. Murphy, "Defending a Juvenile Court Proceeding," 15 *Prac. Law.* 31 (1969).

A. Neigher, "Gault Decision: Due Process and the Juvenile Courts," 31 *Fed. Prob.* 8 (1967).

D. Noonan, "Jury Trials for Juveniles: Toward a More Effective Juvenile Court System," 22 *Syracuse L. Rev.* 780 (1971).

Note, "Admissibility of Juvenile's Statements in Criminal Prosecutions," 36 *Mo. L. Rev.* 382 (1971).

Note, "Constitutional Law—Miranda Warnings to Juveniles in New Jersey: The Worst of Both Worlds Revisited," 26 *Rutgers L. Rev.* 358 (1973).

Note, "Courts, the Constitution and Juvenile Institutional Reform," 52 *B.U.L. Rev.* 33 (1972).

Note, "Discovery Rights in Juvenile Proceedings," 7 *U. San Francisco L. Rev.* 333 (1973).

Note, "Double Jeopardy in Juvenile Justice," 1971 *Wash. U.L.Q.* 702.

Note, "Juvenile Court and Direct Appeal from Waiver of Jurisdiction in Ohio," 18 *Akron L. Rev.* 499 (1975).

Note, "Juvenile Court: Due Process, Double Jeopardy, and the Florida Waiver Procedures," 26 *U. Fla. L. Rev.* 300 (1974).

Note, "Juvenile Due Process Texas-Style: Fruit of the Poisonous Tree Resweetened," 24 *Baylor L. Rev.* 81 (1972).

Note, "Juvenile Law—Double Jeopardy," 8 *U. Richmond L. Rev.* 601 (1974).

Note, "Juveniles and Their Right to a Jury Trial," 15 *Vill. L. Rev.* 972 (1970).

Note, "Problem of Age and Jurisdiction in the Juvenile Court," 19 *Vand. L. Rev.* 833 (1966).

Note, "Prosecutorial Discretion and the Decision to Waive Juvenile Court Jurisdiction," 1973 *Wash. U.L.Q.* 436.

Note, "Review of Improper Juvenile Transfer Hearings," 60 *Va. L. Rev.* 818 (1974).

Note, "Right to Counsel in Virginia Juvenile Proceedings," 3 *U. Richmond L. Rev.* 316 (1969).

Note, "Trial of Juveniles as Adults," 21 *Baylor L. Rev.* 333 (1969).

Note, "Venue in Juvenile Courts," 1973 *Wash. U.L.Q.* 407.

Note, "Waiver in the Juvenile Court," 68 *Colum. L. Rev.* 1149 (1968).

Note, "Waiver of Jurisdiction in Juvenile Courts," 30 *Ohio St. L.J.* 132 (1969).

Note, "Waiver of Jurisdiction in Wisconsin Juvenile Courts," 1968 *Wis. L. Rev.* 551 (1968).

Note, "Waiver of Juvenile Jurisdiction and the Hard-Core Youth," 51 *N.D. L. Rev.* 655 (1975).

S. Novovich, "Constitutional Law: Due Process Requires Proof Beyond a Reasonable Doubt for Juveniles," 7 *Tulsa L.J.* 63 (1971).

M. Ortbals, "Appellate Review of Juvenile Court Proceedings and the Role of the Attorney," 13 *St. Louis U.L.J.* 90 (1968).

G. Parker, "Some Historical Observations on the Juvenile Court," 9 *Crim. L.Q.* 467 (1967).

M. Paulsen, "Kent v. United States: The Constitutional Context of Juvenile Cases," 1966 *Sup. Ct. Rev.* 167.

J. Phillpot, "Jury Trials for Juvenile Delinquents in Virginia," 28 *Wash. & Lee L. Rev.* 135 (1971).

R. Pino, "Polygraph as a Dispositional Aid to the Juvenile Court," 9 *New England L. Rev.* 311 (1974).

A. Platt and R. Freedman, "Limits of Advocacy: Occupational Hazards in Juvenile Court," 116 *U. Pa. L. Rev.* 1156 (1968).

A. Popkin and F. Lippert, "Is There a Constitutional Right to the Insanity Defense in Juvenile Court?" 11 *J. Family L.* 107 (1971).

A. Popkin, F. Lippert, and Keiter, "Another Look at the Role of Due Process in Juvenile Court," 6 *Family L.Q.* 233 (1972).

T. Purdom, "Juvenile Court Proceedings from the Standpoint of the Attorney for the State," 1 *Tex. Tech. L. Rev.* 269 (1970).

W. Ralston, "Intake: Informal Disposition or Adversary Proceedings?" 17 *Crime & Delinq.* 160 (1971).

H. Rankin, "Criminal Procedure—Juries in the Juvenile Justice System?" 48 *N.C.L. Rev.* 666 (1970).

C. Reasons, "Gault: Procedural Change and Substantive Effect," 16 *Crime & Delinq.* 163 (1970).

B. Reid, "Juvenile Waiver: The Inconsistent Standard," 2 *Am. J. Crim. L.* 331 (1974).

D. Roberts, "California Juvenile: His Rights and Remedies," 1 *Pacific L.J.* 350 (1970)

G. Robinson, "Certification of Minors to the Juvenile Court: An Empirical Study," 8 *San Diego L. Rev.* 404 (1971).

J. Rubin, "Constitutional Rights in Juvenile Court," 16 *Clev.-Mar. L. Rev.* 477 (1967).

S. Rubin, "Juvenile Court System in Evolution," 2 *Valparaiso U.L. Rev.* 1 (1967).

D. Rudstein, "Double Jeopardy in Juvenile Proceedings," 14 *Wm. & Mary L. Rev.* 266 (1972).

C. Saylor, "Interrogation of Juveniles: The Right to a Parent's Presence," 77 *Dick. L. Rev.* 543 (1973).

F. Scarpitti and R. Stephenson, "Juvenile Court Dispositions—Factors in the Decision-Making Process," 17 *Crime & Delinq.* 142 (1971).

F. T. Schornhorst, "The Waiver of Juvenile Court Jurisdiction: Kent Revisited," 43 *Ind. L.J.* 583 (1968).

G. Schroeder, "Developments in the Enforcement of Parental and State Standards in Juvenile Proceedings," 10 *Idaho L. Rev.* 153 (1974).

L. Schwerin, "Juvenile Court Revolution in Washington," 44 *Wash. L. Rev.* 421 (1969).

J. Shullenberger and P. Murphy, "Crisis in Juvenile Court—Is Bifurcation an Answer?" 55 *Chi. B. Record* 117 (1973).

D. Skoler, "Counsel in Juvenile Court Proceedings—A Total Criminal Justice Perspective," 43 *Ind. L.J.* 558 (1968).

L. Smith, "Juvenile Right to Bail," 11 *J. Family L.* 81 (1971).

K. Smith, "Profile of Juvenile Court Judges in the United States," 25 *Juv. Justice* 27 (1974).

M. Stamm, "Need for Juvenile Code Revision," 25 *Juv. Justice* 14 (1974).

M. Stamm, "Transfer of Jurisdiction in Juvenile Court: An Analysis of the Proceeding, Its Role in the Administration of Justice, and a Proposal for the Reform of Kentucky Law," 62 *Ky. L.J.* 122 (1973).

G. Strieker, "Waiver of Constitutional Rights by Minors: A Question of Law or Fact?" 19 *Hastings L.J.* 223 (1967).

R. Stubbs, "Role of the Lawyer in Juvenile Court," 6 *Man. L.J.* 65 (1974).

A. Sussman, "Psychological Testing and Juvenile Justice: An Invalid Judicial Function," 10 *Crim. L. Bull.* 117 (1974).

R. Warmuth, "Procedural Due Process in the Juvenile Courts of West Virginia," 76 *W. Va. L. Rev.* 16 (1973).

G. Weinkauf, "Conflict of Parens Patriae and Constitutional Concepts of Juvenile Justice," 6 *Lincoln L. Rev.* 65 (1970).

J. Weyhrich, "Representing the Juvenile in the Adjudicatory Hearing," 12 *St. Louis U.L.J.* 466 (1968).

C. Whitebread and R. Batey, "Juvenile Double Jeopardy," 63 *Geo. L.J.* 857 (1975).

K. Winston, "Self-Incrimination Context: Establishing Procedural Protections in Juvenile and College Disciplinary Proceedings," 48 *S. Cal. L. Rev.* 813 (1975).

L. Wren, "Miranda Doctrine and Juvenile Court," 18 *Juv. Ct. Judges J.* 115 (1968).

W. Zewadski, "Delinquency and Denied Rights in Florida's Juvenile Court System," 20 *U. Fla. L. Rev.* 369 (1968).